GLENCOE LANGUAGE ARTS

VOCABULARY POWER

GRADE 10

Glencoe
McGraw-Hill

New York, New York   Columbus, Ohio   Woodland Hills, California   Peoria, Illinois

To the Teacher

Vocabulary Power is a workbook that offers exercises, skills practice, reviews, and tests to expand student word power and to develop a deeper understanding of language. The vocabulary is selected from a variety of sources, including standardized tests, the *Living Word Vocabulary*, and *Roget's Thesaurus.* Designed to build communication power, *Vocabulary Power* enables students to grow as thinkers, readers, speakers, and writers.

Glencoe/McGraw-Hill

A Division of The McGraw·Hill Companies

Send all inquiries to:
Glencoe/McGraw-Hill
8787 Orion Place
Columbus, Ohio 43240

ISBN 0-02-818256-1

Printed in the United States of America

3 4 5 6 7 8 9 10 108 04 03 02 01

CONTENTS

CONTENTS

Vocabulary Power

Lesson 1 Using Context Clues

Life is full of transitions—changes from one place, condition, or form to another. Each day, you make the transition from sleeping to waking and from home to school. Each year, you change as you learn new things about life and about yourself. Meanwhile, the world around you is changing, too. Have you ever stopped to notice the way the sky changes throughout a single day or an entire season? The words in this list can help you describe transitions.

Word List

brink	disperse	permeate	subtle
chronology	muted	precipitous	zealously
conscientiously	obliterate		

EXERCISE A Context Clues

For each sentence below use context clues, or clues from the surrounding text, to guess the meaning of the boldfaced vocabulary word. Write your definition of the word. Then, look up the word in a dictionary and write its definition.

1. You could hurt yourself badly if you fell off a **precipitous** cliff.

   My definition _____

   Dictionary definition _____

2. Pale pink is a **subtle** color; bright orange is not.

   My definition _____

   Dictionary definition _____

3. If you put a muzzle over a dog's mouth, its bark is **muted**.

   My definition _____

   Dictionary definition _____

4. When the preacher spoke **zealously** about her faith, she inspired her listeners.

   My definition _____

   Dictionary definition _____

5. Spray paint could **obliterate** a message on a road sign.

   My definition _____

   Dictionary definition _____

6. Employees who do their work **conscientiously** are efficient and well-respected.

   My definition _____

   Dictionary definition _____

Vocabulary Power continued

7. A **chronology** of your life lists the main events in the order of occurrence.

My definition _____

Dictionary definition _____

8. When you peel an orange, its scent will quickly **permeate** the room.

My definition _____

Dictionary definition _____

9. Nonstop arguing could bring a couple to the **brink** of breaking up.

My definition _____

Dictionary definition _____

10. In fall, the fluffy seeds of a milkweed pod **disperse** in the wind.

My definition _____

Dictionary definition _____

EXERCISE B Clues Matching
Write the vocabulary word that best matches the clue.

1. Could describe a sharp drop in toy sales. _____

2. Could describe a slightly humorous remark. _____

3. A time line is an example of one. _____

4. Music heard from behind a closed door could sound this way. _____

5. Bombs dropped from an airplane could do this to a bridge. _____

6. Crowds do this after a football game. _____

7. An employee who double-checks all information before putting it into a report is said to work this way. _____

8. A person who passionately pursues something is said to do it this way. _____

9. Food coloring dropped into clear water will do this in the liquid. _____

10. The edge of a steep place. _____

EXERCISE C Usage
Write the vocabulary word that matches each definition.

1. passionately   _____

2. spread throughout   _____

3. with care and thoughtfulness _____

4. break up in random fashion _____

Vocabulary Power

Lesson 2 The Prefixes *inter-* and *intra-*

Prefixes, or syllables attached before a root or base word to alter or enhance its meaning, are important tools for understanding and learning new words. The Latin prefix *inter-* means "between" and the Latin prefix *intra-* means "within." For example, the word *intercollegiate* means "between colleges," and the word *intracollegiate* means "within a college."

Word List

intercom	intermediary	interrogate	intrastate
interject	intermittent	intramural	intravenous
interlaced	interplay		

EXERCISE A Word Association

Read the brief definition of each boldfaced word below. Then, list other words, ideas, or situations you can think of that describe or relate to the vocabulary word.

1. **intramural:** within an institution

   Related words, situations _____

2. **intercom:** device for communicating between rooms

   Related words, situations _____

3. **interlaced:** lacing together; intermixed

   Related words, situations _____

4. **interplay:** back-and-forth action; action and reaction

   Related words, situations _____

5. **intrastate:** within a single state

   Related words, situations _____

6. **interject:** insert between two other things

   Related words, situations _____

7. **intermediary:** person who acts as a go-between, especially to settle differences

   Related words, situations _____

8. **interrogate:** question formally

   Related words, situations _____

9. **intermittent:** stopping and starting at intervals

   Related words, situations _____

♭ *Vocabulary Power* continued

10. **intravenous**: within or into a vein

   Related words, situations _____

EXERCISE B   Usage

If the boldfaced word is used correctly, write *correct* above it. If not, draw a line through it and write the correct vocabulary word above it.

   1. Although it was sunny most of the day, **interlaced** showers dampened the field.

   2. The patient received **intravenous** medication after the operation.

   3. As he worked in the kitchen, Harry used the **interplay** to talk to his brother upstairs.

   4. **Intrastate** packages were shipped by truck from Chicago, Illinois, to Naperville, Illinois.

   5. Before we vote on the matter, I'd like to **interject** a word of caution.

EXERCISE C   Context Clues

Write the vocabulary word that best fits each sentence.

   1. The verbal _____ between the two stand-up comedians was very clever.

   2. Their dialogue was _____ with many references to well-known political figures.

   3. The sophomore Pacers beat the senior All-Stars at the _____ basketball tournament.

   4. Next Tuesday, the senators will _____ several environmental experts on air pollution.

   5. The president of Finland served as the _____ in peace negotiations between the warring parties in Yugoslavia.

   6. Miguel heard a(n) _____ knocking, but each time he went to the door no one was there.

   7. The patient cannot eat solid food right after the operation, so this _____ tube supplies a glucose solution to the bloodstream.

   8. He chose to _____ humorous remarks into serious political commentary.

   9. Indiana University and Purdue University are _____ basketball rivals.

   10. Every morning, our principal makes announcements over the _____.

Vocabulary Power

Lesson 3 Recognizing Base Words and Roots

A base word carries the main meaning of a word. For example, the words *restart* and *startle* share the base word *start*. A root, unlike a base word, cannot stand alone. Many English words have roots that go back to Latin, the language spoken by the ancient Romans. For example, the words *predict* and *dictator* share the Latin root *dict*, which means "say." Recognizing the base word or the root in an unfamiliar word can often help you figure out the word's meaning.

Word List

digression	infamous	retort	torsion
dispassionate	protracted	systematic	traction
disposition	regress		

EXERCISE A Base Words

Each of the boldfaced words below contains a base word that is probably familiar to you. Write the base word. Then, write the dictionary definition of the vocabulary word.

1. dispassionate _____

   Dictionary definition _____

2. infamous _____

   Dictionary definition _____

3. systematic _____

   Dictionary definition _____

4. disposition _____

   Dictionary definition _____

EXERCISE B Word Roots

Write the vocabulary words that share the roots listed. Then, look up the meaning of each word in the dictionary and write its definition.

1. *tort* means "twist"

   _____

   _____

2. *gress* means "go" or "wander"

   _____

   _____

Vocabulary Power *continued*

3. *tract* means "draw" or "pull"

_____

_____

EXERCISE C Context Clues

Answer each question with an explanation. Use your understanding of the boldfaced vocabulary word in your answer.

1. Would a car's tires have good **traction** in deep mud?

_____

2. Is telling a long joke in the middle of a formal speech a **digression**?

_____

3. Is Adolf Hitler regarded as an **infamous** leader?

_____

4. Would the father of someone in a skating competition be a **dispassionate** judge of the performances?

_____

5. Would a **systematic** worker be likely to do a job well?

_____

EXERCISE D Multiple-Meaning Words

Several of the vocabulary words have more than one meaning. Using your understanding of these meanings, write the word that best describes each of the following. Then, write a sentence for each word, using the meaning given.

1. to go back to childhood _____

_____

2. having a disgraceful reputation _____

_____

3. a truck's grip on a muddy road _____

_____

4. relating to the classifying of species _____

_____

5. a person's verbal retaliation in a fight _____

_____

Vocabulary Power

Lesson 4 Using Reading Skills
Learning from Context: Definitions

When you encounter a new word in your reading, you can often use the context, or the surrounding words, to help you guess the word's meaning. Notice that the sentence you just read gives a definition of context. In this case, the word *or* is a clue that a definition or clarification follows. Some other words that signal a definition are *in other words*, *that is*, and *which is*. However, a definition may be given in the context without the use of such clue words.

EXERCISE A Context Clues
In each sentence, underline the part of the sentence that gives a definition of the boldfaced word.

1. The first stop on the city tour is the **arboretum**, a place where many different trees, shrubs, and other plants are grown for scientific and educational purposes.

2. The shop specializes in **nautical** supplies; in other words, it stocks everything relating to ships, sailors, or navigation on water.

3. The band ended its concert with a **medley**, or series, of jazz tunes from the 1930s.

4. The speaker in this poem uses conversational **diction**; in fact, the choice and use of words is much like that of the poet Robert Frost.

5. The expression on her face was **inscrutable**; that is, we found it difficult to interpret.

6. The photograph of the valley was **panoramic**, providing an unbroken view of the entire area.

7. The waters of two rivers **converge** in Pittsburgh, Pennsylvania, where the Allegheny and the Monongahela Rivers come together to form the Ohio River.

8. This springlike weather in early February is **delectable**; I can't remember when the weather was so delightful.

9. To assume a superior manner or to lower oneself to a level considered beneath one's dignity is to **condescend**.

10. The funeral began with the reading of an **elegy**, which is a poem or song expressing sorrow for the dead.

EXERCISE B Context Clues
Write a context sentence for each of the following words. Consult a dictionary if you need to, but express the definition in your own words.

1. inscrutable

_____

_____

2. delectable

_____

_____

Vocabulary Power

Review: Unit 1

EXERCISE A

Circle the word in parentheses that best completes each sentence.

1. The heart monitors in the intensive-care unit emitted reassuring (intramural, intravenous, intermittent) beeps throughout the long night after surgery.

2. Miles has an easy-going (disposition, digression, interplay), while Zelda gets excited over the slightest things.

3. The vibrant reds in the old painting had been (interrogated, muted, interjected) over time by the bleaching effect of the sun.

4. Ms. Jaworsky served as the (intercom, intermediary, chronology) between the two companies that were working out an agreement to merge.

5. Our dog seems to (retort, interject, regress) to the puppy stage whenever he plays with another dog.

6. The threat of a thunderstorm made the crowd quickly (obliterate, disperse, interrogate) to find shelter.

7. Feel free to (interrogate, permeate, interject) any additional comments you'd like to add as we address the group.

8. The inspector knew that the (chronology, traction, brink) of the events eliminated Wilmuth from being a suspect.

9. Richard worked (dispassionately, zealously, intermittently)—eating little and taking only short naps—until all of the flood victims had been relocated.

10. The (muted, systematic, precipitous) climb up the rock left Carol feeling weak and dizzy.

EXERCISE B

Give an example of each idea.

1. an intrastate competition _____

2. a subtle color _____

3. a systematic approach _____

4. an intermittent problem _____

5. a chronology of events _____

6. a quick retort _____

Vocabulary Power

Test: Unit 1

PART A

Circle the letter of the word that best fits each sentence.

1. Erosion from wind and rain could _____ the letters on an old gravestone.
   a. obliterate   **b.** disperse   **c.** regress   **d.** permeate

2. In the middle of his Memorial Day speech, the mayor made a(n) _____ to explain why he got into politics.
   a. chronology   **b.** digression   **c.** intermediary   **d.** retort

3. As the clouds gathered and the day turned less sunny, there was also a(n) _____ change in temperature.
   a. muted   **b.** subtle   **c.** dispassionate   **d.** intravenous

4. Only once during the discussion did the professor from the University of Michigan _____ a remark.
   a. disperse   **b.** obliterate   **c.** retort   **d.** interject

5. The nurse obtained a blood sample using a(n) _____ procedure.
   a. dispassionate   **b.** intravenous   **c.** systematic   **d.** infamous

6. After many years of war, the leaders felt the nation was now on the _____ of a new era of peace and prosperity.
   a. intercom   **b.** brink   **c.** traction   **d.** chronology

7. That _____ company used illegal methods to put its competitors out of business.
   a. muted   **b.** systematic   **c.** intermittent   **d.** infamous

8. The audience enjoyed the _____ between the two rappers as they responded to each other.
   a. intercom   **b.** digression   **c.** interplay   **d.** traction

9. Bob took the engine apart piece by piece in a(n) _____ way.
   a. intermittent   **b.** precipitous   **c.** systematic   **d.** subtle

10. Mr. Kajorski's Independence Day speech was _____ with glowing terms describing his new country.
    a. permeated   **b.** interlaced   **c.** protracted   **d.** dispersed

PART B

Circle the letter of the word that has the same meaning as the boldfaced word or phrase.

1. **interaction**
   a. interplay   **b.** intermediary   **c.** intercom   **d.** disposition

2. **grip**
   a. traction   **b.** brink   **c.** torsion   **d.** chronology

3. **unemotional**
   a. subtle   **b.** infamous   **c.** dispassionate   **d.** muted

Vocabulary Power *continued*

4. spread throughout

    a. obliterate   **b.** regress   **c.** permeate   **d.** interject

5. periodic

    a. intermediary   **b.** intermittent   **c.** intrastate   **d.** intravenous

6. typical mood

    a. digression   **b.** interplay   **c.** disposition   **d.** traction

7. reply quickly or angrily

    a. permeate   **b.** obliterate   **c.** interject   **d.** retort

8. within an institution

    a. intrastate   **b.** infamous   **c.** intravenous   **d.** intramural

9. twisting

    a. traction   **b.** torsion   **c.** interplay   **d.** digression

10. scatter

    a. disperse   **b.** interrogate   **c.** obliterate   **d.** interject

11. sequence of events

    a. torsion   **b.** chronology   **c.** traction   **d.** brink

12. disgraceful

    a. infamous   **b.** interlaced   **c.** intermittent   **d.** protracted

13. muffled

    a. precipitous   **b.** protracted   **c.** muted   **d.** interlaced

14. question

    a. retort   **b.** obliterate   **c.** interject   **d.** interrogate

15. extended

    a. subtle   **b.** muted   **c.** protracted   **d.** infamous

Vocabulary Power

Lesson 5 Using Synonyms

You make choices every day. Some are as simple as whether you will have cereal or toast. Other choices are major ones, such as a choice of career. Still other kinds of choices require that you work with others to arrive at a group choice. For example, when you and your friends go to see a movie, you decide as a group which movie to see. The words in this list relate to making choices.

Word List

convoluted	evade	innocuous	interminable
endorse	giddy	insuperable	wary
enhance	impede		

EXERCISE A Synonyms

Synonyms are words with similar meanings. Each boldfaced vocabulary word below is paired with a synonym whose meaning you probably know. Brainstorm other words related to the synonym and write them on the line provided. Then, look up the vocabulary word in a dictionary and write its meaning.

1. **giddy** : dizzy _____

   Dictionary definition _____

2. **interminable** : endless _____

   Dictionary definition _____

3. **wary** : watchful _____

   Dictionary definition _____

4. **convoluted** : complicated _____

   Dictionary definition _____

5. **evade** : escape _____

   Dictionary definition _____

6. **innocuous** : harmless _____

   Dictionary definition _____

7. **enhance** : beautify _____

   Dictionary definition _____

8. **insuperable** : unconquerable _____

   Dictionary definition _____

Vocabulary Power *continued*

9. **endorse** : approve _____

   Dictionary definition _____

10. **impede** : delay _____

   Dictionary definition _____

EXERCISE B Usage

Complete each sentence with the appropriate vocabulary word.

1. The _____ trail through the woods winds around and around and crisscrosses several times.

2. The heavy traffic on the freeway at five o'clock will _____ our getting to the airport.

3. With summer vacation only a day away, the schoolchildren were _____ with excitement.

4. Because he was smiling as he corrected her, she regarded his remarks as _____.

5. The baseball game, which went into extra innings and lasted over four hours, seemed _____.

6. Negative public opinion about the candidate proved to be a(n) _____ barrier; he lost the election by a large margin.

7. The new lace curtains _____ the light and airy feeling of the sunny room.

8. In the article, Jolene, who represents Students Against Drunk Driving, will _____ the idea of an alcohol-free prom night.

9. By pretending to be sick, Yvonne was able to _____ working on the school clean-up project.

10. Since dark thunderclouds were gathering, we were _____ of going swimming.

Vocabulary Power

Lesson 6 The Prefix *re-*

Prefixes are syllables attached before a root or base word to alter or enhance its meaning. They are important tools for understanding and learning new words. The Latin prefix *re-* means "again" or "back." For example, the word *retry* means "try again" and *recall* means "call back."

Word List

recourse	rejuvenated	repel	resigned
recuperate	remorse	resentment	retract
refute	renowned		

EXERCISE A Prefixes, Roots, and Base Words

Read the brief definition of each boldfaced word. These definitions emphasize the meaning of the prefix and the root or base word. Then, look up the word in a dictionary and write its definition. Finally, use each vocabulary word in a sentence.

1. **rejuvenated:** made young again

   Dictionary definition _____

   Sentence _____

2. **repel:** force back

   Dictionary definition _____

   Sentence _____

3. **refute:** argue back

   Dictionary definition _____

   Sentence _____

4. **retract:** pull back

   Dictionary definition _____

   Sentence _____

5. **resigned:** giving up; accepting; to renounce or relinquish

   Dictionary definition _____

   Sentence _____

6. **resentment:** ill will or rancor directed at a slight

   Dictionary definition _____

   Sentence _____

Vocabulary Power *continued*

7. **recuperate:** become healthy again

Dictionary definition _____

Sentence _____

8. **recourse:** a turning to something

Dictionary definition _____

Sentence _____

9. **renowned:** widely known

Dictionary definition _____

Sentence _____

10. **remorse:** repeated gnawing

Dictionary definition _____

Sentence _____

EXERCISE B **Multiple-Meaning Words**
Circle the word in parentheses that best fits each sentence.

1. She was (rejuvenated, resigned, recuperated) to continuing as vice president of the company until the president got another job.

2. The older man (resigned, renowned, rejuvenated) his life by playing in a softball league.

3. Since the hikers had lost their food, they felt their best (recourse, resentment, remorse) was to take the cut-off trail back to camp.

4. She tried hard to (repel, retract, recuperate) his advances without offending him.

EXERCISE C **Context Clues**
Write the vocabulary word that fits each clue.

1. Get well, please! _____

2. Oh, the guilt! _____

3. What a grudge! _____

4. Fight back! _____

5. Like new! _____

6. I've given up! _____

Vocabulary Power

Vocabulary Power

Lesson 7 The Suffix -ize

A suffix is a word ending that can be added to a word or root that modifies the word's meaning. The Greek suffix -ize means "to become like" or "to treat with." For example, the word *finalize* (*final* + *ize*) means "to become final," and *computerize* (*computer* + *ize*) means "to supply with computers" or "to enter on computer." Words ending in -ize are always verbs.

Word List

centralize	idealize	maximize	rationalize
economize	immobilize	mesmerize	scrutinize
equalize	materialize		

EXERCISE A Context Clues

Use the information given about the base word or root and the meaning of the suffix to come up with a possible definition for each word. Then, look up the vocabulary word in a dictionary and write its meaning.

1. The base word is *equal*.

   Equalize might mean _____

   Dictionary definition _____

2. The base word is *central*.

   Centralize might mean _____

   Dictionary definition _____

3. The base word is *ideal*.

   Idealize might mean _____

   Dictionary definition _____

4. *Maximum* means "the greatest possible quantity or degree."

   Maximize might mean _____

   Dictionary definition _____

5. *Economy* can mean "carefulness in spending money or using resources."

   Economize might mean _____

   Dictionary definition _____

6. *Immobile* means "unable to move."

   Immobilize might mean _____

   Dictionary definition _____

Vocabulary Power *continued*

7. *Scrutiny* means "close examination."

   Scrutinize might mean _____

   Dictionary definition _____

8. *Material* means "having matter or substance."

   Materialize might mean _____

   Dictionary definition _____

9. *Mesmer* is the name of a medical hypnotist from the 1700s.

   Mesmerize might mean _____

   Dictionary definition _____

10. *Rational* means "having the ability to reason."

    Rationalize might mean _____

    Dictionary definition _____

EXERCISE B Usage

Answer each question with an explanation. Use your understanding of the boldfaced vocabulary word in in your answer.

1. Could the repetitious sound and movement of ocean waves **mesmerize** you?_____
   _____

2. Can an elephant **materialize** out of thin air?_____
   _____

3. Does a person tend to **idealize** someone he or she has fallen in love with? _____
   _____

4. Could you **economize** on gas by walking instead of driving to nearby places? _____
   _____

5. Could a person **rationalize** by saying, "I don't really want those juicy-looking grapes that I can't reach. They're probably
   sour anyway." _____

6. When you sign a contract, should you **scrutinize** the fine print? _____
   _____

7. Would buying three lottery tickets **maximize** your chance of winning? _____
   _____

8. Can the threat of a volcanic eruption **immobilize** an area? _____
   _____

Vocabulary Power

Lesson 8 Using Reference Skills
Using a Dictionary: Etymology

Many words in English have their origins in other languages. In the dictionary, the origin of a word is usually given in square brackets at the beginning or end of the definition. Here are several examples.

> **blitz** (blits) *n.* [from German *blitzkrieg* : *blitz*, lightning + *krieg*, war; a sudden, swift military attack, especially involving air and ground weapons together] **1.** A heavy bombardment **2.** An intense campaign **3.** A rush on the passer by the defensive linebackers in football
>
> **ensemble** (än säm′ bəl) *n.* [from Latin *insimul*, at the same time] unit or group of parts that produce a single effect, especially a coordinated outfit or a group of performing musicians
>
> **kowtow** (kaủ′ taủ) *v.* [from Chinese (Mandarin) : *kou*, to knock + *tou*, head] **1.** To seek favor by adopting a servant-like attitude **2.** To kneel and touch the forehead to the ground in expression of deep respect or worship
>
> **zenith** (zē′ nith) *n.* [from Arabic *samt* (ar-ra's), path (over the head)] **1.** Point in the sky that is directly above the observer **2.** Highest point reached by a celestial body in its orbit **3.** Point of highest achievement or greatest power

EXERCISE

Use the sample entries above to answer the following questions about word origins.

1. Which word is derived from Latin? _____ Explain how the meaning of the English word relates to its source. _____

2. *Blitz* is a short form of what German word? _____ What does the longer German word mean?

   _____

3. The election committee for a political candidate might create a media blitz to influence voters. Based on the origin of this word, what might a media blitz be like? _____

4. How do the meanings of the Chinese words *kou* and *tou* help to explain the meaning of the English word *kowtow*?

   _____

5. What basic idea is suggested by the Arabic word that is the source of the English word *zenith?* _____

   _____

Vocabulary Power

Review: Unit 2

EXERCISE A

Circle the letter of the word that best fits the definition.

1. argue to disprove
   a. refute   **b.** repel   **c.** idealize   **d.** endorse

2. too large to overcome
   a. renowned   **b.** wary   **c.** interminable   **d.** insuperable

3. deep regret
   a. recourse   **b.** resentment   **c.** maximum   **d.** remorse

4. hypnotize
   a. economize   **b.** mesmerize   **c.** retract   **d.** enhance

5. reduce spending or avoid waste
   a. recuperate   **b.** endorse   **c.** economize   **d.** retract

6. regard as perfect
   a. idealize   **b.** scrutinize   **c.** endorse   **d.** centralize

7. young again
   a. innocuous   **b.** rejuvenated   **c.** convoluted   **d.** renowned

8. complicated
   a. innocuous   **b.** interminable   **c.** convoluted   **d.** renowned

9. make more beautiful
   a. enhance   **b.** mesmerize   **c.** repel   **d.** impede

10. slow the progress of
    a. maximize   **b.** endorse   **c.** refute   **d.** impede

Vocabulary Power

Test: Unit 2

Part A

Circle the letter of the word that best fits each sentence.

1. The fabric in this rain parka is designed to _____ water.
   a. retract   b. evade   c. refute   d. repel

2. The United States is _____ for its many beautiful national parks.
   a. convoluted   b. renowned   c. innocuous   d. giddy

3. In a baseball game, a batter might feel _____ because of an umpire's bad call.
   a. resentment   b. remorse   c. recourse   d. giddy

4. A stiff cast is used to _____ a broken bone so it can heal.
   a. impede   b. refute   c. immobilize   d. endorse

5. Hannah was stung by Jean's comment, but the others thought it was _____.
   a. interminable b. innocuous   c. insuperable   d. wary

6. Because Celeste had seen bear tracks nearby, she was _____ about leaving the food on the picnic
   table unattended.
   a. giddy   b. renowned   c. wary   d. insuperable

7. Exhausted and outnumbered by enemy soldiers, the troop's only _____ was to retreat.
   a. remorse   b. recourse   c. resentment   d. scrutiny

8. Harriet decided to investigate the candidate before she would _____ him.
   a. enhance   b. impede   c. evade   d. endorse

9. Sam proposed that we _____ the recycling program by having everyone bring cans, bottles, and plastic
   to one location.
   a. mesmerize   b. equalize   c. evade   d. centralize

10. Our vision for a better community will begin to _____ when the new hospital is built.
    a. materialize b. scrutinize   c. idealize   d. mesmerize

11. If you apply for a desirable job three times and are turned down each time, you might feel _____ to the
    fact that you would not get the job.
    a. renowned   b. resigned   c. equalized   d. repeled

12. Annie put a sack of groceries in each arm to _____ the weight distribution.
    a. rationalize b. maximize   c. equalize   d. immobilize

Vocabulary Power *continued*

Circle the letter of the correct definition for each vocabulary word.

1. evade
   a. wash over
   b. send out, usually over the air
   c. avoid, usually by cleverness
   d. vary

2. scrutinize
   a. examine closely
   b. scrub thoroughly
   c. scratch
   d. see

3. maximize
   a. make as small as possible
   b. make equal in size
   c. fascinate or hypnotize
   d. increase to the greatest amount

4. rationalize
   a. give credible but false reasons
   b. present a logical argument
   c. divide into equal parts
   d. apply mathematical reasoning

5. impede
   a. stop
   b. slow down
   c. explode
   d. beg forgiveness

6. enhance
   a. approve or support
   b. increase in beauty or value
   c. avoid or escape
   d. handle carefully

7. recuperate
   a. become wealthy again
   b. become healthy again
   c. become famous again
   d. become young again

8. retract
   a. redraw
   b. grip
   c. take back
   d. pull

Vocabulary Power

Lesson 9 Using Synonyms

In certain parts of the country, people like to say, "If you don't like the weather, just wait fifteen minutes—it'll change!" Sometimes, it seems as though the same thing is true of life. The words in this lesson will help you examine life's twists and turns.

Word List

alluring	flaunt	pestilent	solace
curtail	impetuous	sedate	stagnation
disdain	pervade		

EXERCISE A **Synonyms**

Each boldfaced word below is paired with a synonym whose meaning you probably know. Brainstorm other words related to the synonym and write your ideas on the line provided. Then, look up the vocabulary word in a dictionary and write its meaning.

1. **pestilent** : deadly _____

   Dictionary definition _____

2. **stagnation** : motionlessness _____

   Dictionary definition _____

3. **disdain** : scorn _____

   Dictionary definition _____

4. **pervade** : spread throughout _____

   Dictionary definition _____

5. **impetuous** : reckless _____

   Dictionary definition _____

6. **flaunt** : show off _____

   Dictionary definition _____

7. **sedate** : calm _____

   Dictionary definition _____

8. **curtail** : restrict _____

   Dictionary definition _____

9. **solace** : comfort _____

Vocabulary Power *continued*

Dictionary definition _____

10. **alluring** : attractive _____

Dictionary definition _____

EXERCISE B Multiple-Meaning Words

Some words have several related definitions listed within a single dictionary entry. To explore the multiple meanings of words in the vocabulary list, circle the letter of the item that best completes each statement below. Use a dictionary, if necessary.

1. **Sedate** can mean "to dose with sedatives," but it can also mean _____.

   a. having a birthday party   **c.** influencing others

   b. upset or agitated   **d.** having a quiet, steady attitude

2. **Disdain** can mean "to look on with scorn, " but it can also mean _____.

   a. contempt   **c.** approve of

   b. disorderly   **d.** loss of favor

3. **Solace** can mean "an alleviation of grief or anxiety," but it can also mean _____.

   a. pity or remorse   **c.** when the sun crosses earth's axis

   b. to console or soothe   **d.** to wander aimlessly

4. **Flaunt** can mean "to wave or flutter showily," but it can also mean _____.

   a. to parade or treat contemptuously   **c.** overact in a play

   b. to undermine   **d.** to run incessantly

5. **Pestilent** can mean "destructive of life," but it can also mean _____.

   a. relevant   **c.** causing displeasure or annoyance

   b. persistent   **d.** lending money to relatives

EXERCISE C Usage

Use your understanding of the boldfaced word to answer each question.

1. What do you think is a good way to avoid **stagnation** of your mind? _____

2. What is a personal characteristic you look on with **disdain**? _____

3. What kind of summer vacation would you find the most **alluring**? _____

4. What activity do you wish your school administrators would **curtail**? _____

5. How do you feel when you see someone **flaunt** an accomplishment? _____

Vocabulary Power

Lesson 10 Greek Word Roots

In this lesson, you will learn ten useful English words that are based on roots from the Greek language. Knowing the meanings of Greek roots can help you make an educated guess about the meaning of some new words. Occasionally, however, the exact meaning of the new word isn't clear from the root. It's always safer to look up new words in a dictionary.

Word List

anachronism	euthanasia	hypodermic	psychopath
anthropomorphic	genealogy	periphery	traumatic
dehydration	hierarchy		

EXERCISE A **Analyzing Word Parts**

Read the clues. Then, write in the probable definition of the vocabulary word.

1. *Phery* is a Greek root meaning "carry." *Peri-* is a Greek prefix meaning "around." **Periphery** probably means

_____.

2. *Trauma* is a Greek root meaning "wound." **Traumatic** probably means _____

_____.

3. *Chronos* is a Greek root meaning "time." *Ana-* is a Greek prefix meaning "back." A Greek suffix that creates a

noun is *-ism*. **Anachronism** probably means _____.

4. *Thanatos* or *thana* is a Greek root meaning "death." *Eu-* is a Greek prefix meaning "good" or "well."

Euthanasia probably means _____.

5. *Genea* is a Greek root meaning "race" or "ancestors." A Greek root meaning "word" or "knowledge of" is

ologia. **Genealogy** probably means _____.

6. *Psych* is a Greek root meaning "mind" or "spirit." *Patho* is a Greek root meaning "suffering," "feeling," or

"disease." **Psychopath** probably means _____.

7. *Anthropo* is a Greek root meaning "human." *Morpho* is a Greek root meaning "form." **Anthropomorphic**

probably means _____.

8. *Dermato* is a Greek root meaning "skin." *Hypo-* is a Greek prefix meaning "under." **Hypodermic** probably

means _____.

9. *Hiero* is a Greek root meaning "priestly" or "sacred." *Archy* or *arch* is a Greek root meaning "rule" or

"government." **Hierarchy** probably means _____.

10. *Hydro* is a Greek root meaning "water." *De-* is a Latin prefix meaning "remove." **Dehydration** probably

means _____.

Vocabulary Power *continued*

EXERCISE B Definitions

Check your definitions in Exercise A by looking up each vocabulary word in a dictionary. Write the meaning. How close did you come to the correct meaning?

1. periphery: _____

2. traumatic: _____

3. anachronism: _____

4. euthanasia: _____

5. genealogy: _____

6. psychopath: _____

7. anthropomorphic: _____

8. hypodermic: _____

9. hierarchy: _____

10. dehydration: _____

EXERCISE C Context Clues

Draw a line through the italicized phrase. Above it, write the vocabulary word that best fits the sentence.

1. The clock that chimes in Shakespeare's play, *Julius Caesar,* is a(n) *out-of-its-proper-time-period mechanism* because that kind of clock didn't exist during Caesar's time.

2. "All signs indicate that the writer of these letters is a *severely mentally ill person*," said the police inspector in a worried voice.

3. The first test question was to arrange the animals in a(n) *system ranked with the most important ones at the top.*

4. Have you seen clouds that appeared to be *in human shapes?*

5. The knights marched around the *outer boundary* of the castle, anxiously scanning the horizon for signs of the approaching king.

EXERCISE D Word Webs

On separate sheets of paper, create word webs for three of the vocabulary words in this lesson. Start by drawing a circle with the word in the center. Then, add as many words as you can that have the same Greek root. Quiz a partner about the meanings of the words you add to your web.

Vocabulary Power

Vocabulary Power

Lesson 11 Word Families

Word families are groups of words that contain the same roots or base words. Base words are roots that are complete words. The root or base word gives a word its main meaning. A prefix or suffix combined with the root or base word gives it a different meaning. In this lesson, you will study words in the same word families.

Word List

cognition	elaborate	interrogation	sonorous
corpulent	innovate	sentiment	transcribe
dormant	insoluble		

EXERCISE A Definitions

Look up each of the boldfaced words in a dictionary and write its meaning. Then, use the information in the dictionary entry to underline the root or base word.

1. interrogation: _____

2. cognition: _____

3. elaborate: _____

4. sentiment: _____

5. innovate: _____

6. sonorous: _____

7. transcribe: _____

8. corpulent: _____

9. insoluble: _____

10. dormant: _____

EXERCISE B Word Root Definitions

Write the main meaning of the root or base word for each of the ten vocabulary words introduced in this lesson.

1. roga _____

2. cogn _____

3. labor _____

4. sens, sent _____

5. nova, nov _____

Vocabulary Power *continued*

6. son _____

7. script, scribe _____

8. corp _____

9. sol, solv _____

10. dorm _____

EXERCISE C **Root and Base Words**

Use the chart to write down other words in the word families of the vocabulary words. First, underline the root or base word in the word in the first column. Then, fill in the row with as many other words as you can that contain the same root or base word. Underline the root or base word in each new word after you write it in the space. The root or base word may appear in your new word in slightly different form. You may use a dictionary to find words in the word families.

Word Family Chart

dormant			
insoluble			
cognition			
interrogation			
corpulent			
elaborate			
sentiment			
innovate			
transcribe			
sonorous			

EXERCISE D **Usage**

On a separate sheet of paper, write a sentence of your own for each vocabulary word.

Vocabulary Power

Vocabulary Power

Lesson 12 Using Reference Skills
Using a Thesaurus: Synonyms

A thesaurus (from the ancient Greek word for treasure) is a useful reference work that lists synonyms (and often antonyms) for thousands of words. The synonyms vary slightly in meaning and feeling, so you can find just the right word. To use a thesaurus to find synonyms, first look in an index for the word you are researching. A reference number refers you to a listing in the main part of the thesaurus. The most well-known thesaurus, compiled by Peter Roget (row-ZHAY) in the mid-1800s and since updated by others, is organized in this way. Other thesauruses omit the index. In these, you just look up the word, which will be followed by a list of synonyms, and sometimes, antonyms. In the same way that dictionaries define different meanings of a word, thesauruses list synonyms for each different meaning of a word. In this lesson, you will get practice in using a thesaurus to find synonyms.

EXERCISE

Entries from a thesaurus are listed below. Look over the entries. Then, answer the questions that follow.

> 96 **corpulent** *adj* ample, bulky, chubby, fat, heavy, huge, obese, overweight, plump, portly, round, stout, whopping
> 151 **disdain** *v* be indifferent to, detest, dislike, mock, reject, scorn, take no interest in
> 207 **elaborate** *adj* complex, complicated, decorated, intricate, involved, laborious, ornate, painstaking
> 645 **solace** *n* aid, assistance, alleviation, comfort, consolation, cure, help, relief, respite, sympathy
> 819 **traumatic** *adj* damaging, disabling, disturbing, jolting, shocking, upsetting

1. What does the number in front of each entry probably represent?_____

2. Which synonyms for *elaborate* might you use if you were writing a report about *elaborate* architecture?

   _____

   If you were writing a report about *elaborate* literature? _____

   Explain your answers. _____

3. Which synonym for *traumatic* seems to project the strongest emotion? _____

   The mildest? _____

4. Suppose you are having trouble deciding whether to use alleviation or sympathy as a synonym for *solace*.

   How would you find out exactly how the two words differ in meaning? _____

5. *Disdain* appears here as a verb. The same word can also be a noun. Based on this thesaurus entry, create some

   synonyms for the noun *disdain*. _____

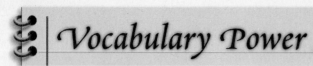
Vocabulary Power

Review: Unit 3

EXERCISE A
Circle the letter of the word that can replace the word or phrase in italics.

1. The teacher explained that my research paper rambled around the *outer boundary* of the subject without ever addressing the real issue.
   a. disdain   **b.** periphery   **c.** hierarchy   **d.** interrogation

2. "This seemingly *impossible-to-solve* problem has stumped the experts for over a century!" the professor exclaimed.
   a. sonorous   **b.** pestilent   **c.** traumatic   **d.** insoluble

3. In the company *ranking system*, Mr. Winkle stood very near the bottom.
   a. euthanasia   **b.** periphery   **c.** hierarchy   **d.** cognition

4. A dreadful smell began to *fill up* the house as the small black-and-white animal lifted and shook its tail.
   a. sedate   **b.** transcribe   **c.** pervade   **d.** flaunt

5. After five days in the desert, the survivors of the plane crash were suffering from *lack of water.*
   a. dehydration   **b.** geneology   **c.** euthanasia   **d.** cognition

6. Maria and Li *show off* their report cards whenever they get A's.
   a. transcribe   **b.** flaunt   **c.** pervade   **d.** curtail

7. That movie about the friendship of a(n) *seriously mentally ill person* and his pet doesn't appeal to me.
   a. hypodermic   **b.** geneaology   **c.** anachronism   **d.** psychopath

8. If we are to stay within our budget, we must *restrict* our spending.
   a. curtail   **b.** flaunt   **c.** pervade   **d.** innovate

9. If the company is to prosper in the coming year, no *reckless* decisions can be made.
   a. dormant   **b.** elaborate   **c.** sonorous   **d.** impetuous

10. Her love for old books and furniture seems like a(n) *thing out of its proper time period* in the ultra-modern house.
    a. anachronism   **b.** sentiment   **c.** stagnation   **d.** pestilent

EXERCISE B
Write sentences using the following vocabulary words.

1. interrogation _____

2. sonorous _____

3. dormant _____

4. transcribe _____

Vocabulary Power

Test: Unit 3

Part A
Circle the letter of the word that best fits the sentence.

1. Many people consider_____and other medical procedures that end life nothing more than murder.
   a. dehydration   **b.** cognition   **c.** euthanasia   **d.** stagnation

2. It was hard to say which delicious item on the dessert buffet table was the most _____.
   a. alluring   **b.** sedate   **c.** pestilent   **d.** impetuous

3. The rank-smelling water at the bottom of the old well was in a state of _____.
   a. anachronism   **b.** disdain   **c.** stagnation   **d.** cremation

4. Three bowls of food every day has made Virginia's dog, Dodo, more than a little _____.
   a. sonorous   **b.** anthropomorphic   **c.** insoluble   **d.** corpulent

5. The doctor used a _____ needle to inject the polio vaccine.
   a. traumatic   **b.** corpulent   **c.** pestilent   **d.** hypodermic

6. The film created in most of the audience a bittersweet _____.
   a. hierarchy   **b.** sentiment   **c.** interrogation   **d.** solace

7. We all felt that Richard's plans for decorating the entryway to the dance floor were far too _____.
   a. elaborate   **b.** pestilent   **c.** sonorous   **d.** hypodermic

8. Discovering the old letters his great-grandmother wrote awoke Jim's interest in his family's _____.
   a. anachronism   **b.** euthanasia   **c.** disdain   **d.** genealogy

9. Science-fiction writers often create aliens with _____ characteristics.
   a. sedate   **b.** anthropomorphic   **c.** corpulent   **d.** dormant

10. The police officer's words were little _____ to the father of the injured girl.
    a. disdain   **b.** cognition   **c.** hierarchy   **d.** solace

Part B
Circle the letter of the word that is most nearly *opposite* in meaning to the boldfaced word.

1. **impetuous**
   a. clever   **b.** frightened   **c.** ridiculous   **d.** cautious

2. **dormant**
   a. lazy   **b.** hard-working   **c.** active   **d.** slow

3. **sedate**
   a. bright   **b.** excitable   **c.** calm   **d.** redundant

Vocabulary Power continued

4. traumatic

   a. comforting   **b.** disturbing   **c.** confusing   **d.** traveling

5. insoluble

   a. puzzling   **b.** small   **c.** friendly   **d.** solvable

Part C

Circle the letter of the word or words that is a *synonym* of the boldfaced word.

1. **psychopath**

   a. mentally ill person   **c.** genius

   b. person out of proper time period   **d.** strange road

2. **pestilent**

   a. insect-like   **c.** lacking water

   b. harmful   **d.** incessant

3. **curtail**

   a. expand   **c.** admire

   b. make longer   **d.** reduce

4. **transcript**

   a. something out of its proper time period   **c.** written record

   b. play   **d.** railway ties

5. **disdain**

   a. approve   **c.** prevent

   b. reject   **d.** reclaim

Vocabulary Power

Lesson 13 Using Context Clues

What does it take to meet life's challenges? What qualities can help you overcome some of the hurdles you might encounter? What are the best ways to address a problem, examine its likely consequences, and then make them work in your favor? The words in this lesson relate to these questions.

Word List

beguile	fortitude	obscurity	sagacious
demure	hidebound	resilient	tumult
equanimity	laud		

EXERCISE A Synonyms

Each boldfaced word is paired with a synonym whose meaning you probably know. Brainstorm other related words and write your ideas on the line provided. Then, look up the vocabulary word in a dictionary and write its meaning.

1. **resilient:** flexible _____

   Dictionary definition _____

2. **sagacious:** wise _____

   Dictionary definition _____

3. **equanimity:** composure _____

   Dictionary definition _____

4. **fortitude:** strength _____

   Dictionary definition _____

5. **obscurity:** vagueness _____

   Dictionary definition _____

6. **beguile:** deceive _____

   Dictionary definition _____

7. **demure:** shy _____

   Dictionary definition _____

8. **hidebound:** narrow-minded _____

   Dictionary definition _____

9. **tumult:** commotion _____

   Dictionary definition _____

Vocabulary Power continued

10. **laud:** praise _____

   Dictionary definition _____

EXERCISE B Context Clues
Answer each question based on your understanding of the boldfaced word.

1. Do you think Michael Jordan spent his basketball career in **obscurity**? Why or why not? _____

2. How do you think a **resilient** person would react to getting a bad grade on a math exam? _____

3. Is it a good characteristic for professional comedians to be **demure**? Explain your answer. _____

4. What is one thing your school does to **laud** students? _____

5. Do you think it would be easy to **beguile** skilled magicians? Why or why not? _____

6. Could a **tumult** occur in your town's sports arena if one of the teams won a championship by one point? Why or why not? _____

7. Name someone you feel is **hidebound**. What evidence do you have for feeling this way? _____

8. If a customer throws a temper tantrum when the clerk overcharges him ten cents, does his behavior show **equanimity**? Explain your answer. _____

9. Is it a **sagacious** decision to jaywalk on a crowded downtown street? Why or why not? _____

10. Which two words in this lesson do you think are nearly opposite in meaning? Explain your answer. _____

Vocabulary Power

Vocabulary Power

Lesson 14 Using Multiple-Meaning Words

As you start new classes, make new friends, move to a new area, or experience inner changes, you let go of the old and encounter the new. You greet the new with a mixture of feelings—forthrightness and uncertainty, fearlessness and fearfulness, attraction and distress. Often, you have help from parents, teachers, other adults, and peers in dealing with new situations. The words in this lesson will help you to understand and express your feelings about these changes in your life.

Word List			
abhor	insinuation	suppress	tribulation
candor	pall	tentative	volatile
dauntless	patronize		

EXERCISE A Multiple-Meaning Words

Some words have several related definitions listed within a single dictionary entry. Look up each boldfaced word in the dictionary and write its meaning(s). Then, write a sentence using one of the definitions for each word.

1. tentative: _____

_____

2. dauntless: _____

_____

3. patronize: _____

_____

4. pall: _____

_____

5. tribulation: _____

_____

6. abhor: _____

_____

7. candor: _____

_____

8. insinuation: _____

_____

Name _____ Date _____ Class _____

9. volatile: _____

_____

10. suppress: _____

_____

EXERCISE B **Sentence Completion**

Write the vocabulary word that best fits each sentence.

1. The candidate's narrow loss threw a _____ over the election night party.

2. The opposing coach's _____ that our players were out of shape was false.

3. We watched as the new calf took its first _____ steps.

4. Northerners and Southerners suffered great _____ during the Civil War.

5. Marcus considers his _____ to be honest and virtuous, but everyone else regards it as rudeness.

6. The brutal dictator tried unsuccessfully to _____ the freedom movement.

7. "I _____ all kinds of cruelty to animals!" the animal-rights speaker proclaimed.

8. Because of Sharon's _____ nature, her friends avoid her when things go badly.

9. The retired chef promised to _____ the new restaurant to help build a customer base.

10. Jeff's dog is _____—he allows no one he doesn't know on the property.

EXERCISE C **Usage**

Below you'll find the titles of five new books. Write a descriptive sentence for each title using a different vocabulary word from this lesson for each one.

1. *Please, Sir, I Want Some More* by Oliver Twist _____

_____

2. *How to Get Rich by Cheating Your Friends and Relatives* by Arnold Worthless _____

_____

3. *My Unhappy Life* by Sylvia Weeper _____

_____

4. *Cooking with Jalapeño Peppers* by Jorge Caliente _____

_____

5. *Hanging Around Famous People* by Ima Toady _____

_____

Vocabulary Power

Vocabulary Power

Lesson 15 Prefixes Meaning "For" and "Against"

Knowing the meaning of prefixes can help you discover the meanings of unknown words. The Latin prefix *pro-* means "for" or "in favor of." The following Latin prefixes mean "against" or "opposed to": *counter-*, *contra-*, or *con-*; *anti-*, and *ob-* or *op-*. These prefixes also have other meanings; not all words that begin with these letter combinations have the meanings of the prefixes.

Word List

antibiotic	contraband	obstruct	oppugn
antipathy	contradictory	obtrude	proponent
antithesis	counterweight		

EXERCISE A Definitions

Underline the prefix in each of the ten boldfaced words. Then, look up the word in a dictionary and write its meaning.

1. obstruct: _____

2. counterweight: _____

3. antipathy: _____

4. oppugn: _____

5. contraband: _____

6. obtrude: _____

7. antithesis: _____

8. antibiotic: _____

9. contradictory: _____

10. proponent: _____

EXERCISE B Context Clues

Write the vocabulary word that best matches the clue.

1. Politicians try to do this to each other's positions on the issues. _____

2. A person who is one of these argues in favor of something. _____

3. You'd look for this if you were a customs agent. _____

4. Doctors and veterinarians use this frequently. _____

5. A big dog in a small hallway can easily do this. _____

6. This allows some types of bridges to be raised. _____

7. Many people have this in regard to snakes and spiders. _____

8. Evidence in a murder trial is often presented in this way. _____

9. A slang synonym for this word is *butt in*. _____

10. In many ways, communism is this when compared with capitalism. _____

EXERCISE C Usage
Write a sentence of your own using each boldfaced word.

1. antithesis _____

_____

2. oppugn _____

_____

3. contradictory _____

_____

4. counterweight _____

_____

5. contraband _____

_____

6. obtrude _____

_____

7. proponent _____

_____

8. antibiotic _____

_____

9. obstruct _____

_____

10. antipathy _____

_____

EXERCISE D Prefixes
Prefixes meaning "for" and "against" appear often in newspapers and magazines. On a separate sheet of paper, make a list of words you find using these prefixes. After each word, use the context or the dictionary to define the word.

Vocabulary Power

Lesson 16 Reading Skills
Learning from Context: Examples

Context, or the environment in which a word appears, can offer many clues to the meaning of an unknown word. One technique is to look for examples of the unknown word that can give a hint about the meaning of the word. For example, imagine that a paragraph describes zebras, pigs, and tigers as quadrupeds and states that humans, insects, and spiders are not quadrupeds. You can use the context clue of examples to figure out that *quadruped* probably means "four-legged." This lesson will give you practice in using examples to find the meanings of unfamiliar words.

EXERCISE A

Read each sentence. Circle the examples that help you define the boldfaced word. Then, write a possible definition of the term on the line.

1. Volunteers for the clean-up crew were as **sparse** as hen's teeth, fish fur, or pig feathers! *Sparse*

    probably means _____.

2. The first **malicious** rumor she spread was that I had cheated on the exam; then, she charged that I had

    used a computer to change my grade! *Malicious* probably means _____.

3. The **wanton** destruction caused by such famous villains as Ghengis Khan and Attila the Hun has gone

    down as the worst in history. *Wanton* probably means _____.

4. The hurricane in Japan was just the latest in a long series of **cataclysms**, including a flood, a volcanic

    eruption, and an earthquake. *Cataclysm* probably means _____.

5. Our team's most **formidable** opponents in the race for the Super Bowl were the Denver Broncos, the San

    Francisco Forty-Niners, and the Green Bay Packers. *Formidable* probably means _____

    _____.

6. For the North, the **nadir** of the Civil War was, no doubt, the crushing defeats at Fredericksburg and

    Chancellorsville in 1862 and 1863, respectively. *Nadir* probably means _____.

7. Jimmy Carter, Ronald Reagan, and George Bush were Bill Clinton's **predecessors** in the White House.

    Predecessor probably means _____.

8. Among the greatest **accolades** authors can receive are the Nobel Prize for Literature, the Pulitzer Prize, and

    the National Book Award. *Accolade* probably means _____.

9. The **opulent** resort featured lavish suites, first-class entertainment and meals, a half-dozen swimming pools,

    and, not surprisingly, sky-high prices. *Opulent* probably means _____.

10. Tourists love Vermont's **picturesque** country villages, old white churches, and small dairy farms with black-

    and-white Holstein cows. *Picturesque* probably means _____.

Vocabulary Power

Review: Unit 4

EXERCISE

Circle the letter of the word that can replace the word or words in italics.

1. Corey's uncle is one of the most *narrow-minded* people I've ever had the displeasure to meet.
   a. resilient   **b.** hidebound   **c.** dauntless   **d.** demure

2. Her *natural dislike* for snakes was made worse when her sister was bitten by a copperhead while on a camping trip.
   a. antibiotic   **b.** antithesis   **c.** antipathy   **d.** candor

3. Everyone knew Sean was *able to bounce back*, but we were all amazed at how quickly he recovered from the accident.
   a. dauntless   **b.** volatile   **c.** sagacious   **d.** resilient

4. At first, the governor's support for the prison reform was *unsure*, but after a few months, her enthusiasm for it increased.
   a. tentative   **b.** resilient   **c.** hidebound   **d.** dauntless

5. Being a former soldier, he was a(n) *strong supporter* of a powerful military.
   a. proponent   **b.** counterweight   **c.** contraband   **d.** antithesis

6. The *uproar* created in the department by the surprise announcement affected morale.
   a. equanimity   **b.** pall   **c.** tumult   **d.** fortitude

7. The chimp looked so ridiculous in the ballerina costume that I couldn't *hold back* my laughter.
   a. abhor   **b.** suppress   **c.** laud   **d.** oppugn

8. "Must you always *force* your way into the conversation? When we want your opinion, we'll ask for it!"
   a. oppugn   **b.** obstruct   **c.** obtrude   **d.** patronize

9. Through her skill and speed, the magician was able to *deceive* the crowd into thinking the motorcycles had disappeared.
   a. beguile   **b.** laud   **c.** suppress   **d.** abhor

10. One of my sisters is quite *shy*, but the other one is a big show-off.
    a. contradictory   **b.** sagacious   **c.** volatile   **d.** demure

Vocabulary Power

Test: Unit 4

Circle the letter of the word that best fits the sentence.

1. "Please don't _____ me, Madam," cried the offended painter. "I don't appreciate being talked down to!"
   a. laud   **b.** patronize   **c.** beguile   **d.** abhor

2. His reasons for making the difficult decision were hidden in _____; we never unearthed them.
   a. obscurity   **b.** counterweight   **c.** equanimity   **d.** fortitude

3. "It is my duty to inform you, sir, that you are under arrest for the smuggling of _____," announced the inspector.
   a. contraband   **b.** fortitude   **c.** insinuation   **d.** obscurity

4. The _____ of the island residents was caused by the hurricane.
   a. candor   **b.** fortitude   **c.** equanimity   **d.** tribulation

5. The researcher announced the discovery of a powerful new _____ for the treatment of pneumonia.
   a. antithesis   **b.** antibiotic   **c.** antipathy   **d.** contraband

6. A deep, dark _____ settled over the crowd as the sun set over the hills.
   a. tribulation   **b.** tumult   **c.** candor   **d.** pall

7. The votes of the liberals must be considered an important _____ to those of the conservatives.
   a. proponent   **b.** fortitude   **c.** counterweight   **d.** antibiotic

8. Amanda became much more _____ about the issue of pollution after her petition was suppressed.
   a. resilient   **b.** volatile   **c.** hidebound   **d.** demure

9. In his argument, Jason presented the complete _____ of the one I had presented earlier.
   a. antipathy   **b.** obscurity   **c.** antithesis   **d.** counterweight

10. When the lawyer continued to make her sarcastic _____ that the witness knew much more than he was admitting, the judge charged her with contempt.
    a. insinuation   **b.** proponent   **c.** tribulation   **d.** tumult

11. "No one enjoys it when you _____ into every conversation, especially when you haven't been asked for your opinion!" I whispered to Melanie.
    a. oppugn   **b.** suppress   **c.** obtrude   **d.** laud

12. Thousands of supporters had gathered at the train station to _____ the soldiers returning after the battle.
    a. laud   **b.** abhor   **c.** patronize   **d.** suppress

13. Your _____ and courage about the matter are certainly refreshing, even if they could get you into trouble!
    a. obscurity   **b.** candor   **c.** proponent   **d.** antipathy

Vocabulary Power *continued*

14. By tackling him, I managed to _____ the robber's escape for a few minutes until the police arrived.
  a. oppugn   **b.** obtrude   **c.** beguile   **d.** obstruct

15. His older sister takes quite an interest in his study of bats, but his younger brothers _____ the winged creatures.
  a. abhor   **b.** suppress   **c.** oppugn   **d.** laud

16. The CEO told the interviewer, "I have never been a _____ of higher corporate taxes, and I do not intend to support them in the future."
  a. counterweight   **b.** contraband   **c.** proponent   **d.** candor

17. The actress did not lose her _____, even when the set collapsed as she was on stage.
  a. candor   **b.** equanimity   **c.** obscurity   **d.** pall

18. The religious leader was well-known for his _____ advice, which he distributed freely.
  a. demure   **b.** resilient   **c.** tentative   **d.** sagacious

19. She was able to _____ others into supporting her get-rich-quick scheme.
  a. beguile   **b.** laud   **c.** obtrude   **d.** suppress

20. The firefighters showed their _____ by reentering the burning building to rescue the child.
  a. contraband   **b.** fortitude   **c.** insinuation   **d.** antipathy

Part B

Circle the letter of the word that is a synonym for the boldfaced word.

1. hidebound
  a. open-minded   **b.** inflexible   **c.** cheerful   **d.** morose

2. antipathy
  a. sympathy   **b.** communication   **c.** dislike   **d.** obscurity

3. tribulation
  a. hardship   **b.** membership   **c.** pride   **d.** concern

4. tumult
  a. stillness   **b.** candor   **c.** display   **d.** disorder

5. oppugn
  a. approve   **b.** criticize   **c.** evaluate   **d.** appreciate

Vocabulary Power

Lesson 17 Using Context Clues

Remembering can involve memorizing information for a test or recalling an event when you smell popcorn or hear a song. Whether you are trying to recover a lost fact or a forgotten name on the tip of your tongue, you are making every effort to locate something that you have stored in your brain. The words in this lesson will help you to write and speak about the process of remembering.

Word List

adept	confound	diligent	tantalize
axiom	cumulative	superlative	unerring
complement	delve		

EXERCISE A Context Clues

Write the vocabulary word that best matches each clue below.

1. This type of person would take the time needed to recall information accurately. He or she is hardworking and careful. _____

2. Mouthwatering cakes and pies displayed behind the window of a closed bakery might do this to some people.

_____

3. This kind of person may not have any difficulty remembering facts, places, or people. He or she is very skilled or proficient. _____

4. Having to spell an unfamiliar word might do this to a contestant in a spelling bee. _____

5. This kind of experience is one you remember because it surpasses all others. _____

6. This information is an established rule, principle, or law that is universally recognized. _____

7. This kind of activity will help uncover information that is deeply buried. _____

8. Your final exam may be considered this when it combines material from last semester with what you have studied this semester. _____

9. This is something that completes something else or brings it to perfection. _____

10. This kind of person is frequently right on target. He or she tends to be sure and exact when doing something. _____

EXERCISE B Multiple-Meaning Words

Consider the multiple definitions of the vocabulary words in the following sentences. Circle the word in each set of parentheses that best completes the sentence.

1. She told Stan he was a(n) (cumulative, axiom, diligent) helper.

2. The Law of Gravity is a(n) (axiom, complement, superlative) that you can easily test for yourself.

Vocabulary Power continued

3. An attractively set table can (delve, confound, complement) a well-prepared meal.

4. Geometry and physics seemed to (tantalize, delve, confound) Martin because he could not visualize what he did not see in front of him.

5. He is considered highly (axiom, adept, cumulative) in his field of psychology.

6. The (complement, axiom, confound) of soldiers marched impressively at his back.

7. In an attempt to (delve, complement, confound) his pursuers, the fugitive swam the river.

8. Joe has often said that attending the rock opera, *Tommy*, was a(n) (unerring, superlative, diligent) experience in the theater.

9. The Marantzes were (adept, unerring, superlative) enough to do the tango but too shy to do it at their daughter's wedding.

10. Many medications have a(n) (adept, superlative, cumulative) effect, because they are stored in the body for several weeks until they start working correctly.

EXERCISE C Usage

Draw a line through the italicized word or phrase. Above it, write the correct vocabulary word that can replace it.

1. Einstein's formula E=MC^2 is a(n) *universally recognized truth.*

2. Genealogists use old diaries and documents to *dig or search* into past and present family connections.

3. Mrs. Jacobson liked to *tease* the cat with chicken and pieces of hot dog.

4. Diving in water with poor visibility can *perplex* even the most experienced divers because it is difficult to distinguish up from down.

5. A 30° angle can *complete* a 60° angle to form a right angle.

6. Once you become *very skilled* at waltzing you will probably not need to count the steps so carefully.

7. Debbie could not think of enough comments that were *superior to all others* to explain her appreciation of the author's discussion.

8. The librarians are looking for *hardworking* volunteers who will not be distracted from their work.

9. Because of Carmichael's dedication and his *faultless* sense of style, the house was gorgeously redecorated.

10. The final exam is not *increasing in size by successive additions;* it covers only the material we have studied this semester.

Vocabulary Power

Lesson 18 Compound Words

Whenever a new invention or a new situation requires a new word to describe it, people often turn to compound words to do the job. A compound word is a word formed from two or more words to express a single idea. Compound words can take one of three different forms: separate words, as in sleeping bag; hyphenated words, as in baby-sitter; and single words, as in turtleneck or onlooker. No simple rule explains the difference. Instead, you need to check a dictionary for the correct form of compound words.

Word List			
backlash	gridlock	superhighway	underdog
benchmark	outsource	tip-off	wind chime
common sense	overkill		

EXERCISE **Context Clues**

Read the sentences below. Then, circle the letter of the correct definition of the boldfaced word.

1. To cut costs, the company chose to **outsource** their software detailing.
   a. transfer data from one location to another
   b. send work to an outside resource
   c. moved employees from one place to another
   d. send workers to lunch

2. Being shorter and lighter than her opponent, Sandy was considered the **underdog** in the wrestling competition.
   a. one that is expected to lose
   b. person who has an advantage
   c. person who draws attention away from the intended issue
   d. at the back of the pack

3. With the school administration refusing to spend any more money and the seniors adamant about needing more decorations for the dance, work on the prom had reached a **gridlock**.
   a. a state of nervous irritability
   b. a complete lack of movement or progress
   c. an informal meeting for the exchange of views
   d. uncertainty in cost limits

4. Eileen was well-known for her **common sense** until she left the car running all night.
   a. sixth sense
   b. confusion
   c. speed
   d. sound judgment

Vocabulary Power *continued*

5. Many people like to travel on a divided **superhighway**, but I prefer the more scenic two-lane roads.
   a. high-speed telecommunication networks that link millions of sources
   b. an expressway that has four or more lanes for traffic
   c. something attached as a permanent appendage or apparatus
   d. a road above all other roads

6. My parents thought the extra banners, giant balloons, and circus clowns were **overkill**, but I liked everything.
   a. more of something than is necessary or appropriate
   b. a superficial impression of brilliance
   c. entirely without fault or imperfection
   d. an action performed perfectly

7. Professor Jeeves collects **wind chimes** from Asian and European countries.
   a. boxes of knicknacks
   b. hanging decorations that make noise when there is a breeze
   c. the sound the wind makes as it passes over pipes
   d. organ pipes and the noises they make

8. Those who had voted for the town pool never imagined the **backlash** from residents who don't use it.
   a. foolish chatter
   b. a place or situation regarded as isolated or backward
   c. an antagonistic reaction to an earlier action
   d. uncertain reaction to an event

9. Detective Smits successfully broke up the smuggling ring with the help of a **tip-off** from one of his most trusted sources.
   a. confidential disclosure
   b. official document issued by city police
   c. written note intended as an explanation
   d. blank piece of paper

10. The quality of Mrs. Monahan's sixth period class projects will serve as a **benchmark** for this class.
    a. something consumed to produce energy
    b. seat for only Mark to sit on
    c. the amount of time between two specified events
    d. a standard in measuring or judging a quality or characteristic

Vocabulary Power

Lesson 19 The Latin Roots *frag* and *fract*

The Latin roots *frag* and *fract* come from the Latin verb *frangere*, which means "to break or shatter." These roots are used in a number of English words. A *fracture*, for example, is a break in bone or cartilage. Something that is *fragile* is easily shattered. All of the words in this lesson have something to do with breaking apart.

Word List			
defray	fragment	infraction	osprey
fractional	frail	infringe	refractory
fractious	fritter		

EXERCISE A Context Clues

Choose the vocabulary word that best matches each clue. Then, on the lines provided, write your own definition of the word and the dictionary definition.

1. This word comes from the Latin *refractus*, meaning "broken up." Although it may be used to describe substances that are difficult to melt, shape, or work with, it is generally used to describe behavior. _____

   My definition: _____

   Dictionary definition: _____

2. This word comes from the Latin *fragmentum*, meaning "a piece broken off." It can be used as a noun or a verb. _____

   My definition: _____

   Dictionary definition: _____

3. This word comes from the Latin *infractus*, meaning "destroyed." If you are guilty of one of these, you may be punished. _____

   My definition: _____

   Dictionary definition: _____

4. This word comes from the Latin *frangere*, meaning "to break or shatter." It is a synonym for *fragile*. _____

   My definition: _____

   Dictionary definition: _____

5. This word comes from the Latin *ossifraga*, meaning "bone breaker." It was mistakenly applied to this bird that eats its catch whole. _____

   My definition: _____

   Dictionary definition: _____

Vocabulary Power *continued*

6. This verb comes from the Latin word *infringere*, meaning "to break off." People who do this to their neighbors' property would not be popular._____

My definition: _____

Dictionary definition: _____

7. This verb comes from the French *fritter*, meaning "fragment" or "to break into small pieces." People who do this are considered to be wasteful._____

My definition: _____

Dictionary definition: _____

8. This word comes from the prefix *de-*, meaning "from" or "off" and the Latin word *fractum*, meaning "broken." A politician needs his campaign contributors to do this._____

My definition: _____

Dictionary definition: _____

EXERCISE B Usage

If the boldfaced word is correctly used in the sentence, write *correct* above it. If not, draw a line through it and write the correct vocabulary word above it.

1. Luanne committed an **infraction** of school policy when she left the building during lunch without permission.

2. Increased property taxes for the next five years will help **fritter** the cost of the new pool.

3. The **refractory** mule planted his feet firmly in the dust and refused to go any farther.

4. By the time all the wedding guests had been served, only a **fragment** of the lavish cake was left.

5. With no structured activities planned for summer, Jill and Mark decided to **infringe** away their time by swimming, bicycling, and watching videos.

6. Recovering from surgery, Grandfather tired easily and looked **frail** for several weeks.

7. By building the fence to enclose their property, the Killiams accidentally **infringed** on the protected wetlands.

8. The twins, who had had a long day, were so **fractional** that they were nearly uncontrollable.

EXERCISE C Shades of Meaning

The synonyms *frail*, *fragile*, and *frangible* all come from the same Latin root. Look up the three words in the dictionary; then, write a paragraph explaining both the similarities and the differences in meaning. Provide example sentences for each word to show its typical usage.

Vocabulary Power

Vocabulary Power

Lesson 20 Using Reference Skills
Using a Dictionary: Multiple Meanings

Many words in the dictionary have more than one definition. When you look up a word, you must decide which definition fits the meaning of the sentence in which the word is being used. The following procedure will help you determine which meaning is most appropriate for your purpose.

1. Read all the definitions in an entry.
2. If there is more than one entry for a word, read each entry completely. Some words are **homographs**—they are spelled the same way but are completely different in meaning, origin, and, sometimes, pronunciation. Homographs have separate dictionary entries, each printed with a raised number. For example, suppose that you do not know what *barrage* means in this sentence.
   A barrage of criticism greeted Anthony as he entered the room.
   When you look up *barrage* in the dictionary, you will find that it is a homograph.
   ¹barrage (bär′ ij) *n.* An artificial obstruction built in a watercourse to increase its depth or to divert its flow.
   ²barrage (bə räzh′) *n.* **1 a** : A heavy curtain of artillery fire directed in front of allies to protect them **b** : rapid, concentrated missile discharge **2** An overwhelming outpouring, as of words.
3. Read the sentence in which you found the word, substituting each definition for the word. The one that makes the most sense is the correct definition:
   An overwhelming outpouring, as of words, greeted Anthony as he entered the room.

EXERCISE

In a dictionary, find the appropriate definition of the italicized word in each of the following sentences. First, write the definition; then, write a sentence of your own in which you use the definition.

1. Not even a new stuffed animal could *console* Damita, who had dropped her stuffed seal out the car window.

   Definition: _____

   Sentence: _____

2. Dad keeps change, maps, and pens in the narrow *console* between the car seats.

   Definition: _____

   Sentence: _____

3. When Sasha is overtired, the dark circles under her eyes stand out against her *pallid* face.

   Definition: _____

   Sentence: _____

4. I used to enjoy that writer's fiction, but his prose has become *pallid* and his characters boring.

   Definition: _____

   Sentence: _____

Vocabulary Power

Review: Unit 5

EXERCISE

Circle the letter of the phrase that best completes each sentence.

1. You might expect a **superlative** meal to be _____.
   a. mediocre in ingredients and preparation
   b. superior in quality and taste
   c. high in fat and carbohydrates
   d. skimpy with only a few dishes

2. Someone might feel sorry for the **underdog** because he or she _____.
   a. is not expected to win
   b. lacks the stamina and courage to win
   c. doesn't know how the game is played
   d. has no desire to win

3. A **fractious** person might be expected to _____.
   a. be good at cooking
   b. leave a party well before it is over
   c. make friends easily
   d. be hard to get along with

4. If you have been **confounded** by a math problem, you _____.
   a. cannot understand the problem
   b. did not try to solve it
   c. finished it quickly
   d. can explain it to others

5. A **diligent** person tends to _____.
   a. give up easily
   b. lose his or her temper frequently
   c. work hard at a challenging task
   d. tell stories to entertain others

6. An **infraction** of the rules at the community center may lead to _____.
   a. more food service
   b. the perpetrators losing privileges
   c. global warming
   d. the opening of additional centers

7. You might use the statistics of a favorite baseball player as the **benchmark** to _____.
   a. rate other players
   b. understand why he entered professional sports
   c. make a lot of money
   d. see the contrast between baseball and football

8. If your club plans to **defray** its operating costs, it intends to _____.
   a. spend them on other necessities
   b. conduct a bake sale to earn money
   c. collect charitable contributions
   d. pay the money for those costs

9. An ice cream store would **tantalize** you because _____.
   a. the prices are so expensive
   b. the employees are helpful
   c. of all the delicious flavors
   d. you are allergic to ice cream

10. An example of a **gridlock** would be _____.
    a. a city map
    b. a distracting noise
    c. one move from winning a chess game
    d. a traffic jam

Vocabulary Power

Test: Unit 5

Part A
Circle the letter of the word that best fits each sentence.

1. Much to the embarrassment of his mother, the _____ child had a tantrum in the middle of the store.
   a. fractious   **b.** common sense   **c.** frail   **d.** unerring

2. At football games, Alan always cheers for the _____, the one who is not expected to win.
   a. fragment   **b.** infraction   **c.** backlash   **d.** underdog

3. Many people use possessions, such as homes, cars, clothing, and jewelry, as the _____ of their success.
   a. overkill   **b.** benchmark   **c.** infraction   **d.** axiom

4. Whenever Gwen was enthusiastic about anything from a vacation to a new article of clothing, she used a(n) _____ in every other sentence.
   a. axiom   **b.** complement   **c.** superlative   **d.** tip-off

5. If you have good grades and superior recommendations, a scholarship is a helpful way to _____ enormous college expenses.
   a. complement   **b.** delve   **c.** infringe   **d.** defray

6. The benefits of exercise are _____, affecting the body gradually over time.
   a. cumulative   **b.** adept   **c.** common sense   **d.** fractional

7. Noah was so _____ at packing boxes that he didn't stop to eat.
   a. fractious   **b.** adept   **c.** diligent   **d.** unerring

8. Dismissal from the team seems like excessive punishment for a(n) _____ like not getting a haircut.
   a. infraction   **b.** backlash   **c.** superlative   **d.** osprey

9. The many twins and triplets in today's elementary schools can _____ even the most observant teachers.
   a. delve   **b.** confound   **c.** infringe   **d.** fritter

10. The family was furious when their great-uncle died and left them only a _____ portion of his enormous estate.
    a. refractory   **b.** commonplace   **c.** cumulative   **d.** fractional

11. Three vegetable dishes, five salads, and four main courses are _____ for a normal family dinner.
    a. overkill   **b.** backlash   **c.** axiom   **d.** benchmark

12. It should be _____ for people to turn off their cellular telephones and beepers while at the movies.
    a. overkill   **b.** gridlock   **c.** common sense   **d.** superlative

13. The storm boasted such strong winds that my brass _____ cracked.
    a. osprey   **b.** underdog   **c.** outsource   **d.** wind chime

Vocabulary Power *continued*

14. There is nothing a mystery fan likes better than the opportunity to _____ into a batch of new facts about a particular case.
    a. outsource   b. delve   c. infringe   d. fritter

15. Pillows and ceramics in different shades of aqua _____ the earth tones in the family room.
    a. confound   b. complement   c. infringe   d. defray

Part B

Circle the letter of the word that means the same as the boldfaced word.

1. **fritter**
   a. help   b. stop   c. waste   d. communicate

2. **gridlock**
   a. standstill   b. corruption   c. promise   d. decision

3. **frail**
   a. stubborn   b. hopeless   c. ready   d. weak

4. **tantalize**
   a. test   b. tempt   c. insist   d. resist

5. **superhighway**
   a. street   b. channel   c. passageway   d. expressway

6. **unerring**
   a. exact   b. shy   c. preventable   d. worthless

7. **refractory**
   a. trite   b. cautious   c. resistant   d. dependable

8. **axiom**
   a. work   b. principle   c. circle   d. permit

9. **adept**
   b. stubborn   b. stupid   c. proficient   d. careless

10. **infringe**
    a. inform   b. occupy   c. linger   d. overstep

Vocabulary Power

Lesson 21 Using Context Clues

By their very nature, human beings strive to push back boundaries and to stretch their minds and bodies into the unknown. Quests and encounters are opportunities to reach, strive, seek, succeed, and even fail. The words in this lesson will help you to share your ideas about different kinds of challenges.

Word List

abyss	equilibrium	grapple	palpable
agenda	expend	ideology	transient
ephemeral	fortuitous		

EXERCISE A Context Clues

For each sentence below, use context clues, or clues from the surrounding text, to determine the meaning of the boldfaced vocabulary word. Write your definition of the word. Then, look up the word in a dictionary and write its definition.

1. To early explorers, the Grand Canyon was a frightening **abyss** that seemed to continue forever.

   Your definition _____

   Dictionary definition _____

2. The committee miscalculated the number of tasks on their **agenda**; instead of needing only an afternoon, they really should have set aside an entire day to cover all of them.

   Your definition _____

   Dictionary definition _____

3. Summer flowers like day lilies and morning glories are surprisingly delicate and **ephemeral**; even when the weather is cool, they do not last long.

   Your definition _____

   Dictionary definition _____

4. People who have been on a boat for an extended period often experience difficulty regaining their **equilibrium** once they return to the land.

   Your definition _____

   Dictionary definition _____

5. After working for hours on her project, Ellie did not have energy to **expend** on her other homework.

   Your definition _____

   Dictionary definition _____

Vocabulary Power *continued*

6. Although we had been separated in traffic, it was **fortuitous** that we reconnected with the Allens at the county fair.

Your definition _____

Dictionary definition _____

7. Midge is finding her part-time job difficult to **grapple** with because of homework, cross-country running, and volunteering at the hospital.

Your definition _____

Dictionary definition _____

8. Political **ideology** has led many groups to leave their homes seeking peace and freedom in foreign lands.

Your definition _____

Dictionary definition _____

9. The child's fear was **palpable** in his wide eyes, shaking limbs, and trembling mouth.

Your definition _____

Dictionary definition _____

10. Very few young people understand how **transient** their youth and energy really are.

Your definition _____

Dictionary definition _____

EXERCISE B **Usage**

Draw a line through the italicized phrase and, above it, write the vocabulary word that can replace the phrase.

1. The discovery of penicillin was *happening by chance;* the staphylococcus germ Dr. Alexander Fleming was cultivating accidentally became contaminated with mold that stopped the growth of bacteria.

2. Denise was relieved to discover that her boredom and listlessness were *only temporary.*

3. As the polls closed, the tension at the senator's campaign center became *obvious.*

4. Tulip magnolias are *lasting for a markedly brief time;* one spring rain scatters the delicate petals.

5. In spite of our efforts to get our recycling drive on the town council's *program of things* to be considered, it may be months before any discussion or voting can take place.

Vocabulary Power

Lesson 22 Using Definitions

Literature is filled with tales of quests. From the lofty search for the Holy Grail by the knights of the Round Table to the tender journey of animal companions attempting to find their way home, characters hunt, explore, seek, scout, and experience. The words in this lesson will help you to dramatize their pursuits and yours.

Word List

fraught	momentum	torrid	vigilant
frivolous	narrate	ultimate	wend
gratify	serendipity		

EXERCISE A Definitions

Circle the letter for the correct definition of the boldfaced word.

1. The football player's **momentum** carried him over the goal line for a touchdown.
   a. teammates   b. personal code   c. impulsive behavior d. force of motion

2. "This undertaking is **fraught** with danger, but if anyone can rescue the princess, it is you, sire," the magician told the prince.
   a. filled   b. turned aside by   c. influenced by   d. encouraged

3. The children stayed close to the path as they **wended** their way through the forest.
   a. lost   b. muddled   c. proceeded along   d. stumbled

4. While most people ignored the sign that read "Serious Requests," hopeful consumers lined up in front of the banner that read "**Frivolous** Wishes."
   a. lighthearted   b. charitable   c. unmistakable   d. familiar

5. Considering that he rarely pays attention to anything other than fish, Lowell's discovery of the gold doubloon while scuba diving in Mexico could be attributed only to **serendipity**.
   a. good eyesight   b. luck   c. careful planning   d. divine protection

6. Lani exhibited the **ultimate** courage when she returned to the burning barn to rescue the kittens.
   a. welcome   b. least possible   c. greatest possible   d. surprising

7. The work of the club members means that the community will have a day-care center, which will **gratify** many club members.
   a. horrify   b. please   c. defeat   d. embarrass

8. Many people in the audience could not determine the point of view from which the story was **narrated**.
   a. brought to a close b. classified   c. expected to begin d. told

9. The **vigilant** security guard noticed the open window and thwarted the burglary.
   a. watchful   b. untrained   c. careless   d. distracted

Vocabulary Power *continued*

10. While some soap opera fans appreciate the complicated story lines, others tune in regularly because of the **torrid** love scenes.

   a. silly   **b.** passionate   **c.** unrealistic   **d.** brave

EXERCISE B   Context Clues

If the boldfaced word is correctly used in the sentence, write *correct* above it. If not, draw a line through it and write the correct vocabulary word above it.

1. It was pure **momentum** that brought the twins together after twenty years of being raised separately.

2. Traveling to Central America is more practical during January and February before the days become too **torrid** for enjoyable exploring.

3. If you are very **frivolous**, you might spot a rare scarlet macaw.

4. Many parents are taking a more active role in what their children do on the computer, censoring games **fraught** with violence.

5. Instead of going straight to dinner, we decided to **narrate** our way through the charming, old streets that surrounded the square.

6. Hector mentally prepared for the **gratified** test of his courage—leaping from the tiny ledge into the rushing water twenty feet below.

7. The court system is filled with **frivolous** lawsuits, such as those brought by prisoners who want better food and more movies.

8. Once the mountain climbers rested in the meadow, they lost their **momentum** and decided not to push on for the peak.

9. As we listened to Maria **narrate** the story of her life, we were struck by the number of coincidences that had influenced her decisions.

10. With the government's help to **gratify** his request, Mr. Sokaler was able to find his daughter.

EXERCISE C   Usage

Many English words derive from place names. Using a dictionary, identify the origin of the word *serendipity*. Write a brief overview of your findings in the space below. Based on this information, explain the modern usage of the word.

_____

_____

_____

_____

Vocabulary Power

Lesson 23 Prefixes That Tell Where

Knowing prefixes that tell *where* can help you build your vocabulary. For example, if you know that the Latin prefix *circum-* means "around" or "about," you can more easily figure out the meaning of *circumference* or *circumnavigate*. When you know that *inter-*, from Middle French and Latin, can mean "between" or "among," you are halfway to understanding words like *intercede* and *intercept*. The Latin prefixes *sub-*, meaning "below," "under," "beneath," or "secondary," and Greek *mid-*, meaning "middle," can be instrumental in understanding such words as *subsequent*, *subservient*, *midsummer*, and *midriff*.

Word List

circumlocution	intersperse	midlife	submerge
circumstance	intervention	subconscious	substandard
interact	midcontinent		

EXERCISE A Context Clues

Choose the word from the word list that best matches each clue. On the lines provided, write the word and your own definition of the word, and then check it against a dictionary.

1. This word combines the prefix *mid-* with the Latin root *continere*, meaning "to hold together." It refers to something that might occur in Europe or Asia. _____

   My definition _____

   Dictionary definition _____

2. In this word, the prefix *sub-* combines with the Latin root *mergere*, meaning "to plunge." It can be used figuratively to describe hiding something from view. _____

   My definition _____

   Dictionary definition _____

3. In this word, the prefix *circum-* is added to the Latin root *loqui*, meaning "to speak." It applies to a comment that is not direct. _____

   My definition _____

   Dictionary definition _____

4. This word blends the prefix *inter-* with the root *venir*, meaning "to come." It can refer to a helpful or harmful action. _____

   My definition _____

   Dictionary definition _____

5. The prefix *sub-* joined with the root *standan*, meaning "to stand," produces a word that has to do with something that is below average. _____

   My definition _____

   Dictionary definition _____

6. When *circum-* is added to the root *stare*, meaning "to stand," the word that results is a synonym for event or condition. _____

   My definition _____

   Dictionary definition _____

7. In this word, the prefix *inter-* is added to the root *spargere*, meaning "to scatter." The word that results is a synonym for sprinkle. _____

   My definition _____

   Dictionary definition _____

8. The prefix *inter-* plus the root *actus*, meaning "doing, act," produces this word, which has to do with people enjoying each other's company and their surroundings. _____

   My definition _____

   Dictionary definition _____

9. When the root *scire*, meaning "to know," is added to the prefix *sub-*, the resulting word has to do with one's level of awareness. _____

   My definition _____

   Dictionary definition _____

10. The prefix *mid-* added to the Old English word *lif*, meaning "continuance," refers to something that may happen when a person is in his or her forties. _____

    My definition _____

    Dictionary definition _____

EXERCISE B   Prefixes

There are many other prefixes that refer to a place or direction. Choose one of the prefixes below and find five words that make use of the prefix. Write a definition for each one; then, use each one in a sentence.

trans- = across   *peri-* = around   *ad-* = to, toward

1. _____

2. _____

3. _____

4. _____

5. _____

Vocabulary Power

LESSON 24 Using Reading Skills
Learning from Context: Contrasts

A sentence that contains an unfamiliar word may also include a word or phrase that is opposite in meaning to the unfamiliar word. This built-in clue is a context clue called contrast or opposition, and it can take one of three forms: an antonym; the words *not, no, no one, nobody,* or *nothing;* or transitional expressions used to signal contrast, such as *although, but, however, nevertheless, rather, in contrast, still, unless, despite,* or *rather than.*

Antonym Diffident as a child, Diane is now self-confident and outgoing.
> *Diffident, self-confident,* and *outgoing* are all adjectives modifying Diane. The opposite of *outgoing* and *self-confident* is *shy. Diffident* is defined as "shy and timid; lacking in self-confidence."

Opposite Words Ralph's attempts to calm union members were misunderstood as escalation, not mitigation.
> The word *not* and the sentence structure tell you that *mitigation* contrasts with *escalation.* If Ralph attempted to calm or to mitigate the situation, then escalation must be the opposite. Escalation is defined as "the action of increasing or intensifying."

Transitional Expressions In spite of agreeing not to censure their colleague, the committee could not endorse his behavior.
> The clues tell you that *censure* and *endorse* are opposites, meaning "to criticize severely; express official disapproval" and "to give approval or support to."

EXERCISE
Use context clues to write your own definition of the boldfaced word. Then, check it against the dictionary definition.

1. Michelle's management style made her firm and decisive, rather than **equivocal**.

   My definition _____

   Dictionary definition _____

2. Unwilling to confront the rumors, J.D. seemed more **disposed** to pretend that they did not exist.

   My definition _____

   Dictionary definition _____

3. No one could say that Liam was humble, for his actions and attitudes were often **pretentious**.

   My definition _____

   Dictionary definition _____

4. Although they had once been financially comfortable, when the store closed, the owner's family became **destitute**.

   My definition _____

   Dictionary definition _____

5. **Emboldened** by the success of her short stories, Lydia worked feverishly on her first novel.

   My definition _____

   Dictionary definition _____

Vocabulary Power

Review: Unit 6

EXERCISE

Circle the letter of the word or phrase that best explains the boldfaced word.

1. If someone's communication style is to use **circumlocutions**, you might expect _____.
   a. few direct expressions
   b. many foreign and technical words
   c. arguments and accusations
   d. word images and figures of speech

2. If you try to regain your **equilibrium** after an embarrassing situation, you are trying to recover your _____.
   a. sense of humor
   b. reputation
   c. sense of values
   d. balance or poise

3. When someone speaks about the **torrid** days of summer, he or she is referring to _____ days.
   a. final
   b. intensely hot
   c. first
   d. rainy and humid

4. An **agenda** is a useful tool because it _____.
   a. keeps people organized and on task
   b. guarantees freedom
   c. keeps people honest
   d. encourages firm decisions

5. A **frivolous** remark is most likely to be _____.
   a. hurtful
   b. sympathetic
   c. inappropriately silly
   d. awkward and hypocritical

6. If something is **interspersed**, it is _____.
   a. arranged in an orderly manner
   b. distributed at intervals
   c. lined up in a row
   d. placed in large clumps

7. A **submerged** rock could be dangerous because it is _____.
   a. sharp and pointed
   b. deep
   c. slippery
   d. covered from view

8. A **fortuitous** event is _____.
   a. planned in advance
   b. accidental
   c. scheduled randomly
   d. a bad omen

9. A roller coaster with **momentum** will _____.
   a. make it easily over the next hill
   b. swerve off the track
   c. stop before the top of the hill
   d. sit at the station

10. A **vigilant** person would be trusted to _____.
    a. disrupt others
    b. watch over someone
    c. entertain others
    d. teach someone

Vocabulary Power

Test: Unit 6

PART A

Circle the letter of the word that best completes each sentence.

1. At certain times in history, the _____ of socialism or communism has appealed to downtrodden people who see it as a chance to get their fair share.
   a. equilibrium   b. midcontinent   c. ideology   d. serendipity

2. The open-water check-out dive is the _____ test of a novice diver's proficiency and confidence in the water.
   a. ultimate   b. torrid   c. interspersed   d. ephemeral

3. Carrie denies her habit, but she obviously has the _____ need and desire to bite her nails.
   a. substandard   b. vigilant   c. frivolous   d. subconscious

4. Phil's many offers of employment force him to _____ with the decision of which job to accept.
   a. interact   b. grapple   c. gratify   d. submerge

5. Parents often find their children's infancy much too _____, and they mourn its passing.
   a. transient   b. fortuitous   c. palpable   d. fraught

6. The roller coaster gained _____ as it sped down into the _____ from which there seemed to be no escape.
   a. agenda, substandard   c. ideology, intervention
   b. momentum, abyss   d. midlife, serendipity

7. Superheroes thrive on situations _____ with danger so that they can flaunt their powers and exercise their skills.
   a. interspersed   b. narrated   c. expended   d. fraught

8. With the Monroe Doctrine, the United States promised not to _____ in the affairs of European nations.
   a. submerge   b. gratify   c. intervene   d. expend

9. Wealth and fame do not result from _____; most people generally have to work for their success.
   a. serendipity   b. momentum   c. agendas   d. ideologies

10. Although most people would have to _____ their way through a maze, using trial and error, some individuals have the ability to choose the correct path immediately.
    a. grapple   b. gratify   c. intersperse   d. wend

11. If the subject of widening Moose Hill Road is not on the city council's _____, the issue will not be discussed in this month's meeting.
    a. equilibrium   b. abyss   c. agenda   d. ideology

Vocabulary Power *continued*

12. "Under no _____ should dogs be allowed to roam free," the dog catcher of Branford is known to insist loudly, even when his views are unpopular.
    a. circumlocution   **b.** ideology   **c.** circumstances   **d.** serendipity

13. Neither teasing nor jokes at her expense could unsettle Nita's _____.
    a. equilibrium   **b.** abyss   **c.** circumstance   **d.** momentum

14. In the *Odyssey*, Homer skillfully _____ the misfortunes of Ulysses after the Trojan War.
    a. grapples   **b.** submerges   **c.** narrates   **d.** wends

15. Someone in a(n) _____ crisis might buy a sports car to feel younger.
    a. torrid   **b.** ephemeral   **c.** fortuitous   **d.** midlife

PART B

For each boldfaced word, circle the letter of the word most nearly *opposite* in meaning.

1. frivolous
   a. serious   **b.** flowery   **c.** pliant   **d.** influential

2. fortuitous
   a. lazy   **b.** heavy   **c.** transparent   **d.** inevitable

3. ephemeral
   a. essential   **b.** constant   **c.** common   **d.** lavish

4. gratify
   a. participate   **b.** honor   **c.** perform   **d.** withhold

5. submerge
   a. devote   **b.** accept   **c.** uncover   **d.** bend

6. circumlocution
   a. conciseness   **b.** conflict   **c.** affection   **d.** privilege

7. vigilant
   a. minor   **b.** sociable   **c.** oblivious   **d.** rare

8. palpable
   a. experienced   **b.** imperceptible   **c.** prominent   **d.** common

9. interact
   a. compromise   **b.** provoke   **c.** enjoy   **d.** withdraw

10. expend
    a. conserve   **b.** entice   **c.** linger   **d.** reminisce

Vocabulary Power

Lesson 25 Using Synonyms

Love, whatever its nature, can be many things—wonderful, bewildering, mysterious, complicated. A powerful life force, love helps to make us who and what we are. Like everything else, however, love does not always run smoothly. Because humans are capable of love, we are also subject to its loss and to the feelings associated with such a loss. The words in this lesson help us to express the lessons that are an integral part of loving.

Word List

revel	solitude	unify	wan
reverie	stalwart	unrequited	whet
rift	suave		

EXERCISE A Synonyms

Each boldfaced vocabulary word below is paired with a synonym whose meaning you probably know. Brainstorm other words related to the meaning of the synonym and write your ideas on the line provided. Then, look up the vocabulary word in a dictionary and write its meaning.

1. **whet** : stimulate _____
   Dictionary definition _____

2. **wan** : pale _____
   Dictionary definition _____

3. **unrequited** : not returned _____
   Dictionary definition _____

4. **stalwart** : strong _____
   Dictionary definition _____

5. **suave** : polished _____
   Dictionary definition _____

6. **solitude** : seclusion _____
   Dictionary definition _____

7. **revel** : party _____
   Dictionary definition _____

8. **reverie** : daydream _____
   Dictionary definition _____

𝒱ocabulary 𝒫ower *continued*

9. **unify** : consolidate _____

   Dictionary definition _____

10. **rift** : break _____

   Dictionary definition _____

EXERCISE B   Usage

Draw a line through the italicized word or phrase and, above it, write the vocabulary word that can replace it.

1. After sharing a bedroom with three sisters, Marilyn appreciated the *isolation* of her own tiny apartment.

2. Allen wrote to his cousin Peter, but nothing he did helped to heal the *break in friendly relations* between them.

3. Holly longed to celebrate New Year's Eve with her love, Gary, but her feelings were *not reciprocated.*

4. "Could you move your car?" the officer asked the driver, who was lost in *a state of abstracted musing.*

5. The smells of garlic and parmesan *stimulated* the appetite of the crowd waiting patiently for the festival to begin.

6. As the personnel director, Mack is looking for a *smoothly agreeable and courteous* salesman.

7. The elaborate floats moved slowly by as residents and tourists *took much pleasure* in the beauty of Mardi Gras.

8. Marcia's already *pallid* face became deathly white as she fainted and fell off her chair.

9. Etienne was a *brave and valiant* knight whose efforts helped to change the course of history.

10. The citizens rallied behind the president as he tried to *join* political divisions.

Vocabulary Power

Lesson 26 The Prefixes *mono-* and *bi-*

When the prefixes *mono-* and *bi-* are combined with a variety of roots, the result is a countless number of new words. For example, the prefix *mono-*, meaning "single," when combined with the root *oculus*, meaning "eye," provides us with the word *monocle*, an eyeglass for one eye. A monogram is the initials of a name combined in a single design. In the same way, the prefix *bi-*, meaning "two," when combined with the root *caput*, meaning "head," produces the word *biceps*, a muscle with two points of origin. All of the words in this lesson share the meaning of "single" or "double."

Word List

bicuspid	bilateral	monolith	monotheism
biennial	bilingual	monologue	monotony
bigamy	monogamy		

EXERCISE A   Definitions

Write the word from the list that best matches each clue. On the line provided, write your own definition of the word; then, check it against the dictionary definition of the word.

1. This word is made up of the prefix *bi-* and the root *gamos*, meaning "marriage." The person involved in this commits a crime. _____

   Dictionary definition _____

2. This word is made up of the prefix *mono-* and the root *lith*, meaning "stone." You might find one of these at Stonehenge in England. _____

   Dictionary definition _____

3. The prefix *bi-* is attached to a root meaning "sharp points." If you had trouble with what this word names, you might see a dentist. _____

   Dictionary definition _____

4. The prefix *mono-* and the root *theism*, meaning "deity," combine to form the word that describes the religion practiced by Muslims, Christians, and Jews. _____

   Dictionary definition _____

5. This word is formed by joining the prefix *bi-* with the root *annum*, meaning "year." It may apply to the lifetime of a plant or the frequency of events. _____

   Dictionary definition _____

6. This word, formed by uniting the prefix *mono-* and the root *logue*, meaning "talk," refers to monopolizing the conversation. _____

   Dictionary definition _____

✣ Vocabulary Power continued

7. Adding the prefix *bi-* to the root *lingua*, or "language," makes a word that refers to something that interpreters need to be.

_____

Dictionary definition _____

8. The prefix *mono-*, when added to the root *tone*, or "sound," applies to the way some people speak.

_____

Dictionary definition _____

9. The prefix *bi-*, plus the root *latera*, meaning "sides," produces a word that can apply to triangles or symmetry.

Dictionary definition _____

10. The prefix *mono-* plus the root *gamos*, meaning "marriage," is the legal relationship most people are familiar with.

_____

Dictionary definition _____

EXERCISE B Usage

If the boldfaced word is correctly used in the sentence, write *correct* above it. If not, draw a line through it and write the correct vocabulary word above it.

1. The orthodontist promised that braces would align my **bicuspids** with the rest of my teeth.

2. The massive obelisk was sculpted from a **monologue**.

3. Students from Asia or South America whose English skills are just developing often benefit from **biennial** classes that reinforce the old language while teaching the new.

4. The ancient Greeks did not believe in **monotheism**; instead, they worshipped various gods and goddesses.

5. Although many bird species have several mating partners throughout their lifetimes, the cardinal practices **bigamy**.

6. Although we celebrate our birthdays each year, my cousin and I like to have a **bilateral** party so that we can see each other's friends and get twice as many gifts.

7. The **monotony** of the announcer's voice put everyone to sleep on a hot Friday afternoon.

8. Comedians who deliver effective and funny **monologues** have to be masters of timing and invention.

9. Israel and Iraq signed a **bilateral** agreement that ensured peace and prosperity for both nations for at least ten years.

10. In the event that Mrs. Cardon's divorce did not go through as planned, she decided to postpone her second marriage for several weeks so that she did not accidentally commit **monogamy**.

Vocabulary Power

Lesson 27 The Roots *string* and *strict*

The Latin word *stringere*, which means "to draw tight" or "to bind," usually appears in English words as the root *strin*. However, it can also be spelled *stra* and *stric*. For example, something that is *astringent* draws together body tissues and stops the flow of blood or other secretions. Something *restricted* is confined within limits. Regardless of their spelling, all the words from this root share a similar meaning, "being pulled together."

Word List

constrain	prestige	stress	stringent
constrict	restraint	stricture	unrestrained
distress	straits		

EXERCISE A   Multiple-Meaning Words

Use context clues to determine which meaning of the boldfaced word is used in each sentence. Then, write the dictionary definition that applies.

1. Julia used her **prestige** to control the meeting, which was threatening to get out of hand.

   Dictionary definition _____

2. Ellen tried to **stress** the importance of algae for the oceanic ecosystem.

   Dictionary definition _____

3. Bee stings cause a **stricture** of Janine's trachea, making it hard for her to breathe.

   Dictionary definition _____

4. Jim practiced an aikido move that was supposed to **constrict** a nerve.

   Dictionary definition _____

5. Computer programmers take advantage of the **unrestrained** proliferation of computer programs.

   Dictionary definition _____

6. My grandmother is very **stringent** with her budget because she is not working.

   Dictionary definition _____

7. The sailor shot flares in the air to communicate the ship's **distress** to any nearby ships.

   Dictionary definition _____

8. The police officer had to put handcuffs on the male suspect to **constrain** him.

   Dictionary definition _____

9. She showed great **restraint** by not retorting to the belligerent salesman.

   Dictionary definition _____

𝒱ocabulary Power *continued*

10. The man in the water was obviously in dire **straits** as he floundered helplessly.

Dictionary definition _____

EXERCISE B   Usage

Circle the word that best completes each sentence. Explain the reasons for your choice.

1. The Cunninghams withdrew their application for membership in the golf and tennis club when they learned about (unrestrained, stringent, strictured) regulations that governed everything from behavior to attire.

_____

2. We had no idea what dire (straits, restraint, prestige) meant until we exceeded our credit card limit, lost our apartment, and couldn't even afford to shop for groceries on a regular basis. _____

_____

3. Rosalie chose to (distress, constrain, constrict) her enthusiasm for her cause at the town meeting when she was confronted by the opposition. _____

_____

4. Rubber bands worn on wrists can be good reminders so long as they are not so tight that they (stress, distress, constrict) blood flow. _____

5. Too many tight deadlines added to Steve's (prestige, restraint, stress). _____

_____

6. The children's (distressed, stringent, unrestrained) laughter is a good sign that they are recovering from their ordeal. _____

7. Connie found the (stress, strictures, prestige) of boarding school unbearable and asked her parents if she could return home. _____

8. Kyle learned how valuable pet (restraint, straits, distress) could be when he saw an unleashed dog bite a child at the park. _____

9. Lucy didn't care about the (distress, prestige, restraint) of designer labels; she just sought well-made clothes that would last for years. _____

10. "We won't cause Mom added (stricture, distress, prestige) on the night before her speech," said Dad. "We'll tell her about the car after the fundraiser." _____

_____

Vocabulary Power

Lesson 28 Using Reading Skills
Connotation

Many words have another kind of meaning beyond their surface meaning. Even a simple color can have a wide range of possible meanings, depending on how it is used. The word *black*, for example, denotes "the darkest color" or "a complete lack of light." Going beyond denotation, or the dictionary definition, you can understand that "black is beautiful" and that operating a business "in the black" is positive, while being the "black sheep in the family" or having a "black heart" is not desirable. This is what is meant by *connotation*—the implied or suggested meaning of a word.

Knowing the connotations of words helps you understand language more fully. All of the following words denote a thoroughfare, yet all have different connotations:

alley	a narrow passage through the middle of a block giving access to the rear of lots or buildings.
boulevard	a broad, often landscaped thoroughfare, named after a notable person or event, and located in an area relevant to the name
road	an open way outside of an urban district, formerly for horseback travel, between distant places or for travelers, vehicles, and animals in rural areas, now used interchangeably for urban and rural thoroughfares
street	a paved public means of access through a city, town, or village with sidewalks, buildings, and availability to traffic

Although the above words have similar denotative meanings, the words have different connotations. For example, referring to the world-famous Champs-Élysées Boulevard in Paris as a "road" would be inappropriate. This landmark consists of palaces and some of the finest hotels and restaurants in the world. Awareness of differences in word meanings can help you in reading, speaking, and writing.

EXERCISE A Usage

Explain the meaning of each sentence based on the connotations and denotations of the boldfaced words.

1. Lynn is a **mediocre** singer. _____

   Lynn is an **average** singer. _____

   Lynn is an **adequate** singer. _____

2. Dwight seems **pleased** with his new car. _____

   Dwight seems **elated** with his new car. _____

   Dwight seems **ecstatic** with his new car. _____

EXERCISE B Word Association

Journalists generally try to be neutral; that is, they avoid words with either strong positive or negative connotations. Novelists and other authors, however, usually want to use words with powerful connotations to evoke certain emotions in their readers. Choose one newspaper story and one page from a favorite novel or short story. On the back of this page, make a list of six words from each piece of writing. Rate the words on the basis of connotation, using plus for positive, minus for negative, or X for neutral.

Vocabulary Power

Review: Unit 7

EXERCISE   Circle the letter of the phrase that best explains the boldfaced word.

1. If you are looking for **solitude**, you are probably in need of _____.
   a. good reading material that will keep you amused
   b. a secluded place where you can have peace and quiet
   c. a low calorie but nutritious meal
   d. a crowded dance floor where you can show off your moves

2. If you purchase a **biennial** magazine subscription as a gift, you can expect that _____.
   a. the magazine will probably go out of business in a few months
   b. the price will go up when it is time for renewal
   c. the recipient will receive the magazine twice a year
   d. the recipient will receive the magazine for two years

3. Clothes that **constrict** your body during hot weather are not advisable because they _____.
   a. bind or squeeze
   b. are too big
   c. are too colorful
   d. absorb too much perspiration

4. People who lose themselves in **reverie** are said to be _____.
   a. unaware of responsibility
   b. unbalanced and overly emotional
   c. daydreamers
   d. gluttons for punishment

5. **Bilingual** books are helpful to someone learning a new language because they _____.
   a. are written in two languages
   b. have study questions that cover all the material
   c. have exciting plots and believable characters
   d. follow a magazine format with many pictures and little writing

6. Someone suffering from the effects of **stress** might experience _____.
   a. a guilty conscience
   b. sore muscles and aching joints
   c. broken promises
   d. sleep and appetite disturbances

7. If you saw a friend looking particularly **wan**, you might _____.
   a. offer him or her a ride
   b. suggest that he or she see a doctor
   c. laugh at his or her facial expression
   d. ignore him or her

8. Readers and viewers of plays can learn much from an actor's **monologue** because this _____.
   a. long speech reveals character
   b. short dialogue moves the action
   c. emotional message is the climax
   d. series of puns lightens the mood

Vocabulary Power

Test: Unit 7

PART A

Circle the letter of the word that best completes the sentence.

1. Rick finds that the _____ of tea parties and formal dances makes for the most interesting photographs.
   a. bicuspid   **b.** monotony   **c.** restraint   **d.** solitude

2. While Leslie benefited from the structured nature of the dance program, she did not enjoy the _____ of the demanding practice scheudule.
   a. strictures   **b.** revels   **c.** straits   **d.** rifts

3. _____ is the most accepted form of marriage in the West.
   a. Monotony   **b.** Solitude   **c.** Reverie   **d.** Monogamy

4. In Edgar Allan Poe's "The Mask of the Red Death," the characters _____ at a costume ball until the clock strikes midnight and a surprise guest arrives.
   a. whet   **b.** revel   **c.** constrain   **d.** constrict

5. Even though it was not carved from a single block of stone, the Washington Monument is considered a _____ because it is a tall, thin column.
   a. monolith   **b.** stalwart   **c.** solitude   **d.** restraint

6. Not being able to find his father caused the young boy much _____.
   a. prestige   **b.** reverie   **c.** monotony   **d.** distress

7. After ten days of sightseeing in New York City, Kim was happy to return to the _____ of her house in the countryside, where she could hear the birds sing.
   a. stricture   **b.** solitude   **c.** monogamy   **d.** reverie

8. Enamel seems to wear off each _____ because of the wear and tear during eating and brushing.
   a. bicuspid   **b.** stricture   **c.** rift   **d.** monolith

9. The cruise ship was forced to detour around the _____, which had been narrowed considerably by heavy silt deposits during the storm.
   a. monotony   **b.** straits   **c.** solitude   **d.** monolith

10. _____ is not present in Hinduism since the religion recognizes a multitude of deities.
    a. Monotheism   **b.** Monogamy   **c.** Strictures   **d.** Reverie

11. Alicia dozed in her chair, caught halfway between sleep and _____.
    a. stress   **b.** distress   **c.** prestige   **d.** reverie

12. The _____ in their relationship would take years to heal.
    a. whet   **b.** monologue   **c.** rift   **d.** reverie

Vocabulary Power *continued*

13. The _____ education requirement has been changed in our school district so that all immigrants take an intensive English course.

   a. unrequited   **b.** bilingual   **c.** stringent   **d.** bilateral

14. Some plants are considered _____ because they live for just two years.

   a. suave   **b.** unrestrained   **c.** biennial   **d.** wan

15. Not only was the former police chief charged with fraud, but he was also accused of _____: he had three families in three different cities.

   a. bigamy   **b.** monogamy   **c.** stress   **d.** reverie

PART B

Circle the letter of the word that means most nearly the *opposite* of the boldfaced word.

1. **whet**
   a. depress   **b.** excite   **c.** bend   **d.** influence

2. **suave**
   a. legible   **b.** positive   **c.** uncouth   **d.** handsome

3. **restraint**
   a. memory   **b.** freedom   **c.** respect   **d.** perfection

4. **monotony**
   a. uncertainty   **b.** illumination   **c.** guarantee   **d.** diversity

5. **prestige**
   a. disgrace   **b.** bewilderment   **c.** confidence   **d.** elegance

6. **wan**
   a. unnatural   **b.** ruddy   **c.** calm   **d.** obedient

7. **constrict**
   a. extinguish   **b.** disguise   **c.** loosen   **d.** promise

8. **rift**
   a. unification   **b.** falsehood   **c.** sanctuary   **d.** severity

9. **monologue**
   a. argument   **b.** conversation   **c.** lecture   **d.** compliment

10. **bilateral**
   a. square   **b.** triangular   **c.** two-dimensional   **d.** one-sided

Vocabulary Power

Vocabulary Power

Lesson 29 Using Multiple-Meaning Words

Who are you—a son, a student, a sister, a customer, an athlete, a friend? Your identity depends not only on the behavioral and personal characteristics that define your individuality but also on the times in which you live and the people whom you meet. The words in this lesson will help you to identify, understand, and express the parts of your life that affect who you are.

Word List

disillusion	esteem	manipulate	temperate
dynamic	impressionable	naive	virtuoso
eccentric	invincible		

EXERCISE A Multiple-Meaning Words

Some words have several related definitions listed within a single dictionary entry. Read the sentences below; then, circle the letter of the correct definition of the boldfaced vocabulary word.

1. After climbing the face of Mt. Coria and rappelling down the back side, Gretchen felt **invincible**.

   a. intensely excited

   b. incapable of being overcome or defeated

   c. worthy of imitation

   d. liable to change

2. William Randolph Hearst was once considered **eccentric** because of his collection of wild animals.

   a. concerned with the ordinary and practical

   b. being the only one of its kind

   c. departing from an established norm

   d. having great stature or enormous strength

3. The book about Pacific cultures will **disillusion** Mary, who had hoped to find unsophisticated groups untouched by the West.

   a. deprive of a false or erroneous belief

   b. establish exact limits for

   c. make cross or discontented

   d. cause to have a prejudiced view

4. In order to be a successful entertainer, a person should have a **dynamic** personality.

   a. nervous and impatient

   b. marked by intensity and vigor

   c. difficult to understand

   d. lacking in discipline

5. Historian Barbara Tuchman is **esteemed** for both her scholarship and her writing style.

   a. called attention to boastfully

   b. accused with evil intent

   c. regarded with respect

   d. set forth for consideration

6. The tourists were **naive**, believing that there were bargains still to be found in London flea markets.

   a. showing resourcefulness in difficult situations

   b. lacking experience or judgment

   c. lacking social grace

   d. recklessly wasteful

7. Despite his addiction to video games, Steve maintained a **temperate** diet and a regular exercise schedule.

a. involving moderation and self-restraint

b. designed to shock or thrill

c. marked by eagerness

d. without exception or qualification

8. She was considered a violin **virtuoso** at a very young age.

a. eccentric player

b. convincing performer

c. hesitant performer

d. excellent performer

9. Craig tried his best to **manipulate** the system so that he would be pitted against the weakest golfers, but his attempts were soon discovered.

a. seize by force or authority

b. subject to uniformity

c. tamper with for personal gain

d. substitute for another

10. Wendy was such an **impressionable** young woman that she tended to believe anything she was told.

a. modest and reserved in manner and behavior

b. easily influenced or convinced

c. moodily introspective

d. having no imperfections

EXERCISE B   Synonyms and Antonyms

Circle the letter of the word that has the meaning that is the same as (a synonym) or opposite to (an antonym) that of the vocabulary word.

1. **manipulate:** (synonym)

a. handle   b. expose   c. withdraw   d. grieve for

2. **disillusion:** (antonym)

a. arrange   b. satisfy   c. enchant   d. pierce

3. **temperate:** (synonym)

a. exaggerated   b. moderate   c. unfamiliar   d. qualified

4. **naive:** (antonym)

a. sophisticated   b. biased   c. open   d. inferior

5. **impressionable:** (synonym)

a. broad-minded   b. gullible   c. immature   d. proper

6. **eccentric:** (antonym)

a. calm   b. appropriate   c. unashamed   d. ordinary

7. **dynamic:** (synonym)

a. sneaky   b. active   c. merciless   d. impatient

8. **invincible:** (antonym)

a. vulnerable   b. wise   c. useful   d. anguished

Vocabulary Power

Lesson 30 Using Context Clues

As we progress from infancy toward old age, we continually experience change. Who we are is constantly refined and redefined. That's why the passage from youth to maturity may be less a matter of age than a journey from unknowing into awareness, or from innocence into experience. The words in this lesson will help you to express different facets of the search for identity.

Word List

accentuate	nonchalant	pensive	perseverance
affront	obnoxious	perception	stupor
animated	passive		

EXERCISE A Context Clues

Write the vocabulary word that best matches each clue below.

1. If someone intentionally insults you, he or she would be guilty of committing this._____

2. A person who is lively and spirited._____

3. This kind of person might be found daydreaming about tomorrow's problems._____

4. A person might be in this state if he or she gets bad news or a terrible shock._____

5. This person accepts things without objection or resistance._____

6. Someone who is coolly unconcerned about appearance could be described with this adjective._____

7. The person who has this never gives up, regardless of how difficult things may be._____

8. A person who emphasizes the good points of something does this to the positive._____

9. Few people want to spend time with someone like this who talks loudly and says offensive things._____

10. Everyone has highly individual reactions to experiences due to this, brought to each person through his or her senses._____

EXERCISE B Usage

If the boldfaced word is correctly used in the sentence, write *correct* above it. If not, draw a line through it and write the correct vocabulary word above it.

1. Noel enjoys the **obnoxious** prank of calling people on the telephone and hanging up when they answer.

2. The survivors of the bus accident stood around in a **perception**, their eyes dazed and empty.

Vocabulary Power *continued*

3. Although they tend to look sad and depressed, **passive** people are just wistful; sometimes they get so lost in their thoughts that they neither see nor hear others.

4. Miss Peabody viewed the use of slang and idioms as a personal **affront** to her dignity.

5. Ryan pretends to be **nonchalant** about his scholarship to Yale Drama School, but he is really totally ecstatic.

6. Nadia's **perception** and patience make her the perfect person to input the records into the computer; she will barely take a break until she completes her task.

7. "But that's just your **stupor**, Ed," said Jill impatiently. "You may not understand the entire story about the Chinese farmers because you were raised in a different country and social class."

8. Some would say that **passive** people are easy to get along with, while others see them as easy to control.

9. An **animated** smile spread across Del's face and his eyes sparkled with good humor and excitement.

10. The speaker **accentuated** the first syllables of all his words, creating a strange verbal rhythm.

EXERCISE C Synonyms

Circle the letter of the word that means most nearly the same as the boldfaced word.

1. perseverance
   a. power   b. laziness   c. normality   d. persistence

2. nonchalant
   a. unconcerned   b. noisy   c. uncomfortable   d. tempted

3. affront
   a. surprise   b. management   c. insult   d. torrent

4. pensive
   a. thoughtful   b. nauseous   c. angry   d. guilty

5. stupor
   a. crisis   b. daze   c. outcome   d. habit

6. obnoxious
   a. harmful   b. efficient   c. objectionable   d. willful

7. accentuate
   a. evaluate   b. criticize   c. emphasize   d. legislate

8. animated
   a. lively   b. uncertain   c. excellent   d. prescribed

9. perception
   a. agreement   b. dilemma   c. inclination   d. awareness

10. passive
    a. sickly   b. inactive   c. vibrant   d. disdainful

Vocabulary Power

Lesson 31 The Roots *nym* and *nom*

Both the Greek root *nym* and the Latin root *nom* mean "name" or "word." Thus, the English word *synonym* is built from the prefix *syn-*, meaning "same" or "similar," and *onymum*, meaning "name." As you know, a synonym has the same or nearly the same meaning as another word. In the same way, the English word *nominate* comes from the Latin *nomen*, meaning "name," and is defined as "to propose by name as a candidate, especially for election." The words in this lesson share a common derivation and meaning.

Word List

anonymous	homonym	nomenclature	pseudonym
antonym	ignominy	nominal	renown
denomination	misnomer		

EXERCISE A Etymology

Choose the word from the list that best matches each clue. On the lines provided, write your own definition of the word and the dictionary definition.

1. This word comes from the prefix *mis-*, meaning "wrongly," and the root *nomen*. Iceland and Greenland are two examples of this.

   My definition _____

   Dictionary definition _____

2. The combination of the prefix *pseudo-*, meaning "false," and the root *nomen* produces this word that an author might choose to protect his or her identity.

   My definition _____

   Dictionary definition _____

3. This word derives from the root *nomen* in combination with the word *calare*, meaning "to call." You might use this system in biology class.

   My definition _____

   Dictionary definition _____

4. The prefix *anti-*, meaning "against," and the root *nomen* produce a word applied to pairs, such as high and low.

   My definition _____

   Dictionary definition _____

5. Built from the prefix *de-*, meaning "from," and *nominare*, meaning "to call," this word might apply to a stack of one-dollar bills.

   My definition _____

   Dictionary definition _____

Vocabulary Power continued

6. This word comes from the prefix *homo-*, meaning "same" or "like," and the root *nomen*. These words are spelled the same but have different meanings.

   My definition _____

   Dictionary definition _____

7. This word comes from *nominalis*, meaning "of names." The Queen of England is this kind of leader.

   My definition _____

   Dictionary definition _____

8. Referring to an unknown, this word comes from the prefix *an-*, meaning "without," and *unuma*, meaning "name."

   My definition _____

   Dictionary definition _____

9. Built from the prefix *re-*, meaning "anew," and the root *nomer*, meaning "to name," this word categorizes people like Michael Jordan and Madeleine Albright.

   My definition _____

   Dictionary definition _____

10. This word comes from the prefix *in-*, meaning "not," and the root *nomen*, meaning "name." This word involves a ruined reputation.

    My definition _____

    Dictionary definition _____

EXERCISE B Usage
Underline the word in parentheses that correctly completes each sentence.

1. Mrs. Hughes decided that the (antonym, pseudonym, homonym) game was perfect for trips in the car; thinking of opposites would certainly keep her two children and their friends busy.

2. The bald brother of the Three Stooges was given the (pseudonym, nomenclature, misnomer), "Curly."

3. It took Rafi several weeks to familiarize himself with the (denomination, renown, nomenclature) of computer programming.

4. Lutheranism is a (nomenclature, homonym, denomination) of the Protestant religion.

5. The (anonymous, renown, nominal) caller tipped off the police that a crime was about to take place.

6. The charitable deeds of the land developer won him (ignominy, renown, nomenclature) that lasted for decades.

Vocabulary Power

Lesson 32 Using Reference Skills
Using the Thesaurus: Antonyms

In addition to providing a list of synonyms, or words that mean the same or nearly the same as another word, some thesauruses also provide a list of antonyms. Look at the following modified entries from a thesaurus.

KNOWLEDGE
  I. **Nouns**. cognizance, acquaintance, information, know-how; learning, erudition, wisdom, experience, sophistication.
  II. **Verbs**. know, perceive, discern, recognize, see, comprehend, understand, realize, appreciate, fathom, experience.
  III. **Adjectives**. aware, appreciative, conscious, cognizant, conversant, familiar, informed, alert, apprised, abreast, sensible, alert to, erudite.

  See also DISCOVERY, EXPERIENCE, FAME, INFORMATION, INTELLIGENCE, INTUITION, LEARNING, TEACHING, UNDERSTANDING, WISDOM. *Antonyms*—See IGNORANCE, INEXPERIENCE.

Checking both synonyms and antonyms in a thesaurus can help you to develop your vocabulary and your writing skills. Words with opposite meanings increase your awareness of how language is used. Using antonyms in the right place can clarify meaning, help create an image, or emphasize a point, as these examples show.

  The king rewarded conformity, not disobedience.
  The new baby appeared delicate next to her older and more robust cousin.

EXERCISE

Using a thesaurus, find five synonyms and five antonyms for the word *defiance* to fill in the word web below.

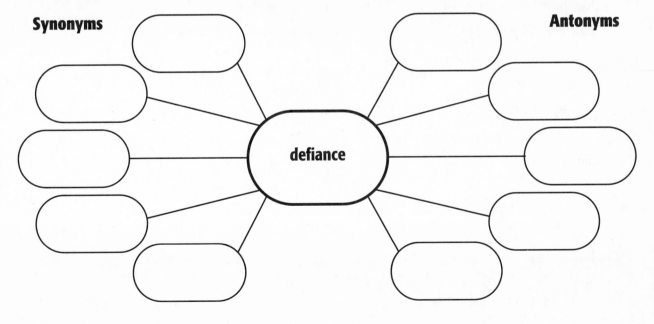

Vocabulary Power

Review: Unit 8

EXERCISE

Circle the letter of the word or phrase that best explains the boldfaced vocabulary word.

1. If someone has a reputation for being **impressionable**, you might expect her to be _____.
   a. conceited and difficult to get along with for extended periods
   b. easily fooled by appearance
   c. hopelessly depressed
   d. uncertain about her future

2. Someone's **perception** of a situation is bound to be different from yours because _____.
   a. of the way people interpret sensory stimuli
   b. of the way the senses defy accuracy
   c. people always agree on what they see and hear
   d. the senses of taste and touch are less well developed than the other senses

3. A writer might adopt a **pseudonym** if _____.
   a. he or she enjoys being recognized
   b. he or she wants a large garden
   c. he or she needs the manuscript edited
   d. he or she wants to try out a new writing style

4. **Obnoxious** people probably have few friends because they _____.
   a. have poor communication skills
   b. tend to offend other people
   c. cannot be honest
   d. are conscious of their social status

5. The name "Hope" seems like a **misnomer** for someone who is as _____.
   a. dejected as she is
   b. intelligent as she is
   c. uncooperative as she is
   d. elegant as she is

6. An **invincible** hero is a person who tends to be _____.
   a. more literary than real-life
   b. conniving, sneaky, and unkind
   c. easily lost and frustrated
   d. brave, strong, and undefeated

7. **Dynamic** characters are more interesting than flat characters because dynamic characters _____.
   a. change and grow
   b. treat others poorly
   c. are the same at the end as they are at the beginning of a story
   d. are modeled after people that the author actually knows

Vocabulary Power

Test: Unit 8

PART A

Circle the letter of the word that best completes the sentence.

1. To give himself the freedom to try different genres without influencing his audience, author Stephen King sometimes writes under the _____ Richard Bachman.
   a. homonym   **b.** pseudonym   **c.** perception   **d.** stupor

2. It's incredibly frustrating to argue with a(n) _____ person because he or she refuses to participate.
   a. demure   **b.** eccentric   **c.** anonymous   **d.** passive

3. The instructor was hard on her film students in order to shatter their incorrect _____ of the film industry.
   a. perceptions   **b.** dynamics   **c.** virtuosos   **d.** affronts

4. AnneMarie's _____ was infectious; anyone who spent an hour with her was invigorated and enthusiastic.
   a. pensiveness   **b.** animation   **c.** eccentricity   **d.** perseverance

5. The agency is looking for a(n) _____ employee to contribute new ideas and change old procedures.
   a. eccentric   **b.** nonchalant   **c.** dynamic   **d.** ignominious

6. Sisyphus, a character in Greek literature, is a model for _____; each time he rolls a large rock to the top of a hill, it rolls down, and he must start anew.
   a. demureness   **b.** perseverance   **c.** esteem   **d.** passiveness

7. As a temporary employee, Sandy has to learn a different _____ for each new job.
   a. nomenclature   **b.** pseudonym   **c.** perception   **d.** renown

8. I'd like to introduce you to my colleague of _____, about whom you have heard so much.
   a. passive   **b.** impressionable   **c.** obnoxious   **d.** renown

9. Lucy checks every _____ to find out what the writer meant.
   a. pseudonym   **b.** misnomer   **c.** stupor   **d.** homonym

10. For his part in finding the wallet, Glen received a(n)_____ reward.
    a. ignominious   **b.** nonchalant   **c.** nominal   **d.** animated

11. Carpal tunnel syndrome, in which the nerves in the wrists and hands are damaged, causes difficulty in the _____ of an object like a computer mouse.
    a. manipulation   **b.** perception   **c.** nomenclature   **d.** homonym

12. "Lucky" was an unfortunate _____ for a dog that had been hit by a truck and lost by an airline.
    a. homonym   **b.** perseverance   **c.** misnomer   **d.** ignominy

Vocabulary Power *continued*

13. People with eye problems sometimes lose their _____ of depth, distance, and space.
    a. nomenclature   b. dynamic   c. misnomer   d. perception

14. Having won all of their games for the past two seasons, the team believed they were _____.
    a. passive   b. invincible   c. temperate   d. naive

15. Audrey and James have the same religion, but each belongs to a different _____.
    a. antonym   b. denomination   c. manipulation   d. perception

PART B

Circle the letter of the word that means most nearly the *opposite* of the boldfaced vocabulary word.

1. **eccentric**
    a. bold   b. hesitant   c. conventional   d. lost

2. **nonchalant**
    a. indifferent   b. formal   c. sickly   d. worried

3. **renown**
    a. goodness   b. humor   c. laziness   d. obscurity

4. **dynamic**
    a. lethargic   b. energetic   c. alone   d. relaxed

5. **affront**
    a. faze   b. compare   c. compliment   d. describe

6. **stupor**
    a. reason   b. animation   c. coma   d. plan

7. **anonymous**
    a. poor   b. weak   c. rigorous   d. known

8. **temperate**
    a. unrestrained   b. hateful   c. angry   d. clear

9. **accentuate**
    a. de-emphasize   b. comprehend   c. complicate   d. destroy

10. **antonym**
    a. pseudonym   b. misnomer   c. synonym   d. homonym

Vocabulary Power

Lesson 33 Using Synonyms

When you walk out your front door in the morning, what do you see, hear, and smell? When you have an argument or a conversation with a friend, how do you feel? Our language is filled with words to describe every detail of our surroundings, the people we know, and the feelings or thoughts that we have. Learning new descriptive words can help to express feelings and observations in the most vivid, specific ways possible. The words in this list relate to observations and expressions.

Word List

aesthetic	gaudy	obtuse	resplendent
balmy	grotesque	poignant	wanton
benign	mundane		

EXERCISE A Synonyms

Each boldfaced word below is paired with a synonym whose meaning you probably know. Brainstorm other related words or situations and write them on the line provided. Then, look up the vocabulary word in a dictionary and write its meaning.

1. **poignant** : moving _____

   Dictionary definition _____

2. **benign** : favorable _____

   Dictionary definition _____

3. **grotesque** : abnormal _____

   Dictionary definition _____

4. **gaudy** : flashy _____

   Dictionary definition _____

5. **balmy** : mild _____

   Dictionary definition _____

6. **resplendent** : brilliant _____

   Dictionary definition _____

7. **obtuse** : rounded; dull-witted _____

   Dictionary definition _____

8. **mundane** : common _____

   Dictionary definition _____

9. **aesthetic** : beautiful _____

   Dictionary definition _____

Vocabulary Power continued

10. **wanton** : reckless _____

Dictionary definition _____

EXERCISE B Usage

Draw a line through the italicized phrase. Above it, write the vocabulary word that can replace the phrase.

1. A *strange and distorted* statue stood on the lawn outside the vacant house.

2. Their first meeting was tense and uncomfortable, but their last two meetings were *friendly and pleasant.*

3. The talented designer's *artistic and elegant* creations impressed the guests at the fall fashion review.

4. We decided that the flowered wallpaper was too *bright and showy* for our simple tastes.

5. The art was supposed to be new and fresh, but I found it quite *ordinary.*

6. Some people wept at the *emotional and heartfelt* tribute to the victims.

7. After a very cold winter, we appreciated yesterday afternoon's *warm and fair* conditions.

8. The driver sped through the narrow streets with a *willful and careless* disregard for pedestrians and other drivers.

9. The joke was not clever, but *confusing and rather unintelligent.*

10. Tourists always looked forward to *bright and intense* sunsets over the water.

EXERCISE C Antonyms

Write the vocabulary word that is opposite in meaning.

1. hurtful _____
2. unemotional _____
3. tasteful _____
4. unique _____
5. beautiful _____

6. quickwitted _____
7. harsh _____
8. faded _____
9. tasteless _____
10. restrained _____

EXERCISE D Multiple-Meaning Words

To explore the multiple meanings of words in the vocabulary list, select the word that correctly completes each statement below. Use a dictionary, if necessary.

1. Her _____ perfume wafted through the airplane, overpowering me six rows away.

2. The _____ climate of Spain was great for Larry's lungs.

3. By giving her child anything he wanted, he had grown _____ in his teenage years.

4. The _____ drawings on the cave walls in Italy were painted by ancient cave dwellers.

5. She tried hard to emulate the modernist _____ of Pablo Picasso.

Vocabulary Power

Lesson 34 Malapropisms

Have you ever confused two words that sound alike? This isn't hard to do—in the English language many words look and sound alike but are completely unrelated in meaning. *Malapropism* is a term that describes the misuse, especially the humorous misuse, of certain words. The list below contains pairs of words often used in malapropisms.

Word List			
anecdote	epitaph	progeny	vivacious
antidote	epithet	reprehend	voracious
apprehend	prodigy		

EXERCISE A Context Clues

For each sentence below, use context clues to determine the meaning of the boldfaced word. Write your definition of the word. Then, look up the word in a dictionary and write its definition.

1. My great-grandparents are proud of their **progeny**, which include four generations.

   My definition _____

   Dictionary definition _____

2. The child pianist, who performed in packed concert halls, was regarded as a musical **prodigy**.

   My definition _____

   Dictionary definition _____

3. Not only were his actions not praised, but one opponent even labeled him with an insulting **epithet**.

   My definition _____

   Dictionary definition _____

4. The poet was asked to write an **epitaph** for the great leader's tombstone.

   My definition _____

   Dictionary definition _____

5. She began her graduation speech by telling an **anecdote** about a personal high school experience.

   My definition _____

   Dictionary definition _____

6. Scientists worked to develop an **antidote** to the poison.

   My definition _____

   Dictionary definition _____

Vocabulary Power *continued*

7. Police officers hoped to **apprehend** the bank robbery suspects before the end of the day.

My definition _____

Dictionary definition _____

8. In public reports, environmentalists have begun to publicly **reprehend** businesses that pollute waterways.

My definition _____

Dictionary definition _____

9. Guests admired their **vivacious** host, who welcomed, greeted, and introduced people all night.

My definition _____

Dictionary definition _____

10. The cooks could hardly make enough food to satisfy the **voracious** appetites of the volunteer workers.

My definition _____

Dictionary definition _____

EXERCISE B Word Association
For each group of words, write the vocabulary word that belongs.

1. genius, intellect, wonder   _____

2. memorial, monument, remembrance   _____

3. remedy, cure, medicine   _____

4. name, slur, insult   _____

5. grab, capture, catch   _____

6. energetic, lively, active   _____

7. offspring, family, descendants   _____

8. accuse, blame, criticize   _____

9. story, tale, narrative   _____

10. greedy, starved, devouring   _____

EXERCISE C Usage
Sometimes, actors and comedians deliberately use malapropisms to make audiences laugh. With a partner, use a separate sheet of paper to write a short skit that uses some of the malapropisms above in humorous ways. Think about humorous and confusing situations that could arise if people do not communicate clearly or if they say one thing but mean something completely different. If you think of any additional words that might make for humorous malapropisms, feel free to add them to your skit.

Vocabulary Power

Lesson 35 The Greek Roots *chron* and *micro*

The root *chron* comes from the Greek word *chronos*, which means "time." The root *micro* comes from the Greek word *mikros*, which means "small." You can use your understanding of these roots to figure out the meanings of a variety of words. The words in the following list contain the root *chron* or *micro*.

Word List

chronic	chronological	microfilm	synchronicity
chronicle	microbe	microscopic	synchronize
chronograph	microbiology		

EXERCISE A   Context Clues

For each sentence below, use context clues to determine the meaning of the boldfaced word. Write your definition of the word. Then, look up the word in a dictionary and write its definition.

1. She was upset to learn that she had a **chronic,** not temporary, condition.

   My definition _____

   Dictionary definition _____

2. We decided to start at the beginning and explain events in **chronological** order.

   My definition _____

   Dictionary definition _____

3. At the festival, it is a tradition to **synchronize** the start of the music with the opening of the fireworks display.

   My definition _____

   Dictionary definition _____

4. Students put together a **chronicle** of the school from its earliest days to the present.

   My definition _____

   Dictionary definition _____

5. They will use some type of **chronograph,** such as a stopwatch, to analyze the speed of their equipment.

   My definition _____

   Dictionary definition _____

6. The **synchronicity** of having several family members receive good news at the same time made us feel lucky.

   My definition _____

   Dictionary definition _____

Vocabulary Power continued

7. At the library, we found some of the magazines in print and some on **microfilm.**

   My definition _____

   Dictionary definition _____

8. In **microbiology,** Lena analyzes organisms that cause certain diseases.

   My definition _____

   Dictionary definition _____

9. Back at the lab, we will study some of the **microscopic** animal life in the pond water.

   My definition _____

   Dictionary definition _____

10. The doctor was able to isolate the **microbe** that was causing the illness.

    My definition _____

    Dictionary definition _____

EXERCISE B Usage

Circle the letter of the word or phrase that best completes each sentence.

1. To illustrate chronological order, you might use a _____.
   a. microscope   **b.** stopwatch   **c.** time line   **d.** road map

2. A person most likely to need a chronograph would be a _____.
   a. clerk   **b.** runner   **c.** mail carrier   **d.** map maker

3. A type of microbe is a _____.
   a. germ   **b.** clock   **c.** microscope   **d.** small mammal

4. A chronic disease is one that _____.
   a. strikes quickly and severely then disappears   **c.** is easily cured in a short amount of time
   b. recurs and lasts a long time   **d.** is usually not noticeable

5. A good example of a chronicle is a _____.
   a. short poem   **b.** history book   **c.** scale   **d.** meter

6. You might synchronize _____.
   a. a disease   **b.** two books   **c.** two watches   **d.** a germ

7. You are most likely to find microfilm _____.
   a. in a library   **c.** on the surface of a pond
   b. in a test tube   **d.** at a track meet

Vocabulary Power

Lesson 36 Using Reference Skills
Using a Dictionary: Homographs

A homograph is a word that is spelled like another but that has a different meaning, origin, and, sometimes, pronunciation. Unlike multiple meanings of the same word, homographs are listed as separate entries in a dictionary. Look at the sample entries below for the word *fret*.

The multiple meanings are related by origin and meaning and are listed in the same entry. Homographs, on the other hand, have separate origins and meanings and have separate entries in a dictionary.

> **fret**[1] (fret) *vt.* [ME (Middle English) *freten*<OE (Old English)<*fretan*, to devour] **1.** to eat away; gnaw **2.** to wear away by gnawing or rubbing **3.** to form by wearing away **4.** to make rough **5.** to annoy or worry–*vi.* **1.** to gnaw **2.** to become eaten or worn **3.** to become disturbed **4.** to become annoyed–*n.* **1.** a wearing away **2.** a place that is worn **3.** an annoyance
>
> **fret**[2] (fret) *n.* [ME *frette*, probably from OFr (Old French) *frete*, interlaced work, with OE frætwa, ornament] **1.** an ornamental net, often worn by women as a headdress **2.** an ornamental pattern of small bars that join at right angles, used as a border or decoration
>
> **fret**[3] (fret) *n.* [OFr *frette*, a band] **1.** any of several narrow ridges across the neck and fingerboard of a banjo, guitar, or other similar stringed instruments to regulate fingering– *vt.* **1.** to press strings against a fret **2.** to place frets on an instrument

EXERCISE A

Write five sentences using the word *fret*. Three of your sentences should demonstrate the meanings of the three homographs, and two of your sentences should show multiple meanings of the same homograph.

1. _____

2. _____

3. _____

4. _____

5. _____

EXERCISE B

Consult a dictionary to find homographs and multiple meanings of the following words. For each homograph, list origins, multiple meanings, and parts of speech.

1. calf _____

2. bow _____

3. hop _____

4. hold _____

5. lap _____

Vocabulary Power

Review: Unit 9

EXERCISE A

Circle the letter of the word that means the *opposite* of the boldfaced word.

1. balmy
   a. dull   **b.** frigid   **c.** uncertain   **d.** harmless

2. wanton
   a. disorderly   **b.** brilliant   **c.** quiet   **d.** careful

3. obtuse
   a. sharp   **b.** simple   **c.** impressive   **d.** complicated

4. vivacious
   a. angry   **b.** greedy   **c.** old   **d.** lazy

5. apprehend
   a. criticize   **b.** tire   **c.** lose   **d.** grasp

6. poignant
   a. quiet   **b.** boring   **c.** entertaining   **d.** emotionless

7. mundane
   a. temporary   **b.** unique   **c.** painful   **d.** simple

8. prodigy
   a. family   **b.** genius   **c.** dullard   **d.** friend

9. resplendent
   a. cold   **b.** complicated   **c.** intelligent   **d.** gloomy

10. chronic
    a. small   **b.** comfortable   **c.** short-lived   **d.** painful

EXERCISE B

Circle the word in parentheses that best completes each sentence.

1. They had to (chronicle, synchronize, reprehend) their watches for the game.

2. There was a (chronic, grotesque, microscopic) film of soap over the lens.

3. My (chronograph, microfilm, microbe) has a light and stopwatch as well.

4. Grandmom's (progeny, antidote, anecdote) had us falling off our chairs laughing.

5. Please arrange these phone calls in (chronological, microscopic, benign) order.

Vocabulary Power

Test: Unit 9

PART A

Circle the letter of the word that best completes each sentence.

1. My grandfather told an interesting _____ about growing up on a farm.
   a. antidote   **b.** progeny   **c.** anecdote   **d.** prodigy

2. Because of his _____ appetite, the family's grocery bills were usually quite high.
   a. voracious   **b.** resplendent   **c.** vivacious   **d.** gaudy

3. One gifted student was labeled a(n) _____, destined for success.
   a. synchronicity   **b.** prodigy   **c.** epithet   **d.** epitaph

4. The ache in her knee was _____ and affected her most on cold or damp mornings.
   a. obtuse   **b.** chronological **c.** chronic   **d.** benign

5. For the funeral, family members created a(n) _____ that would be engraved on a plaque.
   a. chronicle   **b.** epithet   **c.** chronograph   **d.** epitaph

6. A degree in _____ would allow him to study organisms in bodies of water.
   a. microfilm   **b.** microbiology   **c.** synchronicity   **d.** chronograph

7. We used a _____ to measure our running time before the big track meet.
   a. chronograph   **b.** synchronicity **c.** microbe   **d.** prodigy

8. The teacher told us to arrange our essays in a folder in _____ order.
   a. microscopic   **b.** obtuse   **c.** chronic   **d.** chronological

9. For the surprise party, we will have to _____ our arrival times so that everyone is present before the guest of honor arrives.
   a. chronicle   **b.** chronograph   **c.** synchronize   **d.** microbe

10. The explosion was loud but _____, as it didn't cause any damage.
    a. chronic   **b.** resplendent   **c.** grotesque   **d.** benign

PART B

For each boldfaced word, circle the letter of the word that is most nearly *opposite* in meaning.

1. **microscopic**
   a. immense   **b.** scattered   **c.** complicated   **d.** long

2. **aesthetic**
   a. smooth   **b.** unsightly   **c.** frightening   **d.** unfit

3. **gaudy**
   a. tasteful   **b.** old   **c.** polite   **d.** orderly

Vocabulary Power *continued*

4. **balmy**

   a. simple   **b.** wet   **c.** humid   **d.** cold

5. **resplendent**

   a. dull   **b.** stormy   **c.** lively   **d.** small

6. **grotesque**

   a. intelligent   **b.** beautiful   **c.** hopeless   **d.** simple

7. **poignant**

   a. small   **b.** unemotional   **c.** complicated   **d.** tasteful

8. **obtuse**

   a. dull   **b.** intelligent   **c.** cloudy   **d.** minute

9. **reprehend**

   a. praise   **b.** insult   **c.** avoid   **d.** capture

10. **wanton**

    a. intelligent   **b.** foolish   **c.** reckless   **d.** careful

PART C

Circle the letter of the word or phrase that best completes each sentence.

1. A mundane job would probably _____.

   a. bring fame   **c.** be routine and ordinary

   b. be exciting   **d.** require special and rare equipment

2. Being labeled with an epithet is likely to make someone feel _____.

   a. appreciated   **c.** honored

   b. hopeful   **d.** hurt

3. A vivacious person is likely to _____.

   a. be stricken with illness   **c.** have a great deal of energy

   b. be a genius   **d.** eat too much

4. You are most likely to see progeny at a _____.

   a. family reunion   **c.** science conference

   b. business meeting   **d.** library

5. A chronicle of a town _____.

   a. builds its homes   **c.** tells its history

   b. establishes its government   **d.** studies its recent illnesses

Vocabulary Power

Lesson 37 Using Synonyms

When you think of the word *loyalty*, what words and images come to mind? Perhaps you think about good friends who always stand up for one another. You might think of a soldier who fights for his or her country. You might think of a business, cause, or product that you like to support. The words in the following list relate to the idea of having, showing, or experiencing loyalty.

Word List

absolve	comrade	kindred	partisan
advocate	delude	martyr	prevail
benefactor	fidelity		

EXERCISE A   Synonyms

Each boldfaced vocabulary word below is paired with a synonym whose meaning you probably know. Brainstorm other words related to the meaning of the synonym and write your ideas on the line provided. Then, look up the word in a dictionary and write its meaning.

1. **absolve** : forgive _____

   Dictionary definition _____

2. **prevail** : overcome _____

   Dictionary definition _____

3. **delude** : mislead _____

   Dictionary definition _____

4. **comrade** : companion _____

   Dictionary definition _____

5. **fidelity** : faithfulness _____

   Dictionary definition _____

6. **kindred** : related _____

   Dictionary definition _____

7. **advocate** : supporter _____

   Dictionary definition _____

8. **martyr** : victim _____

   Dictionary definition _____

9. **partisan** : one-sided _____

   Dictionary definition _____

Vocabulary Power continued

10. **benefactor** : helper _____

  Dictionary definition _____

EXERCISE B Usage

Draw a line through the italicized word or phrase. Above it, write the vocabulary word that can replace the word or phrase.

1. Her *person conferring a benefit* spoke to her about going to New York City for an art opening.

2. Even during difficult times, I could always count on support from my *close friend.*

3. The ex-con decided to *deceive* the cops by stealing a driver's license.

4. The worshippers pledged *faithfulness and loyalty* to their religion and to their community church.

5. Some believed that members of the House of Representatives voted in a *biased* manner.

6. The soldiers faced a difficult challenge, but they vowed to *control the situation.*

7. When the organization needed support, leaders turned to a well-known *promoter* of their cause.

8. At the trial, the defendants were confident that the jury would *completely clear* them of all guilt.

9. According to legend, Joan of Arc was a *person who sacrificed her life* for her beliefs.

10. They realized that they were *closely related* spirits when it came to their values and interests.

EXERCISE C Word Association

For each group of words, write the vocabulary word that belongs.

1. forgive, pardon, clear _____

2. associate, friend, partner _____

3. bluff, betray, deceive _____

4. truth, steadfastness, faithfulness _____

EXERCISE D Multiple-Meaning Words

Write the vocabulary word that best describes each of the following people or situations.

1. how well a stereo reproduces sound _____

2. similar in spirit or character _____

3. supporter of a cause _____

4. to triumph over a difficulty _____

5. a person assigned to harass an enemy _____

Vocabulary Power

Vocabulary Power

Lesson 38 Using Context Clues

The opposite of loyalty is betrayal. What words and images do you think of when you picture a person abandoning someone or something? Different reasons are involved in acts of betrayal, and such acts have a variety of consequences. The words in the list below all relate to betrayal in some way.

Word List

arrogance	founder	repulse	sordid
caustic	ostentatious	solitary	treachery
disconsolate	predator		

EXERCISE A Context Clues

Each of the following sentences contains context clues that can help you with the meanings of the boldfaced word. Write what you think the word means. Then, look up the word in a dictionary and write its meaning.

1. A spy posed as a loyal subject to the king. When the king learned of this **treachery**, he punished the spy severely.

   My definition _____

   Dictionary definition _____

2. **Arrogance** led the young woman to believe she didn't need friends or associates in her life.

   My definition _____

   Dictionary definition _____

3. His theft of money from the company is likely to **repulse** many fellow workers.

   My definition _____

   Dictionary definition _____

4. Firing the entire staff was an **ostentatious** display of power by the new office manager.

   My definition _____

   Dictionary definition _____

5. The **sordid** tale of her decline from heiress to homeless beggar became a bestseller.

   My definition _____

   Dictionary definition _____

6. Though trained to perform in a circus, the tiger was still considered a **predator**.

   My definition _____

   Dictionary definition _____

7. The ship began to **founder** in the rough sea.

My definition _____

Dictionary definition _____

8. When their key player signed with another team, the athletes were **disconsolate**.

My definition _____

Dictionary definition _____

9. Since he was used to a **solitary** existence, the elderly man had trouble dealing with large crowds.

My definition _____

Dictionary definition _____

10. The judge leveled a **caustic** attack at the lawyers and their inconclusive evidence.

My definition _____

Dictionary definition _____

EXERCISE B Context Clues

Write the vocabulary word that best matches the clue.

1. This word describes the existence of a person who is always alone. _____

2. Actions that are vile and shameful are described in this way. _____

3. A sharp and stinging remark can be described as this. _____

4. This word describes a person who is beyond comfort. _____

5. Something disgusting or highly offensive might affect you in this way. _____

EXERCISE C Word Association

For each group of words, write the vocabulary word that belongs.

1. collapse, fall, sink   _____

2. boastful, loud, glittery   _____

3. stalker, enemy, hunter   _____

4. pride, self-importance, smugness   _____

5. dishonesty, falseness, corruption   _____

EXERCISE D Word Sketch

Each of the vocabulary words expresses a strong emotion or idea. On a separate sheet of paper, create a sketch that illustrates one of the words.

Vocabulary Power

Lesson 39 Prefixes e- and ex-

The prefixes *e-* and *ex-* are related and usually mean "out," "beyond," "away from," or "upward." The Latin prefix *e-* is usually used before the letters *b, d, g, j, l, m, n, r,* or *v.* You can use your understanding of these prefixes to figure out the meanings of a variety of words, including those in the following list.

Word List

elicit	empower	exhilarate	exposition
eminent	evocative	expertise	expunge
emit	excise		

EXERCISE A Prefixes and Meanings

Use both your understanding of the prefixes *e-* and *ex-* and the context of each sentence to determine the meanings of the boldfaced words below. Use a dictionary to check your understanding of each word; then, write its dictionary meaning.

1. They knew something was wrong with the car when it began to **emit** an acrid smell.

   My definition _____

   Dictionary definition _____

2. The reporter tried to **elicit** information from people working on the case, but no one would divulge any.

   My definition _____

   Dictionary definition _____

3. Having worked in many animal shelters, she is regarded as an **eminent** authority on stray animals.

   My definition _____

   Dictionary definition _____

4. We believe letting him complete the task on his own will **empower** him to take control of his life.

   My definition _____

   Dictionary definition _____

5. The **evocative** movie stirred strong feelings among those who remembered World War II.

   My definition _____

   Dictionary definition _____

6. The surgeon decided to **excise** the diseased part of her foot.

   My definition _____

   Dictionary definition _____

Vocabulary Power *continued*

7. The **exposition** of the novel spelled out details of the story's main characters.

My definition _____

Dictionary definition _____

8. They are willing to **expunge** the crime from his record if he does community service for two years.

My definition _____

Dictionary definition _____

9. I guarantee that a ride in the fresh air on a sailboat will **exhilarate** you.

My definition _____

Dictionary definition _____

10. The piano teacher shared his musical **expertise** with his students.

My definition _____

Dictionary definition _____

EXERCISE B Antonyms

Circle the letter of the word that most clearly means the *opposite* of the boldfaced word.

1. emit
   - **a.** scatter
   - **b.** order
   - **c.** discharge
   - **d.** gather

2. empower
   - **a.** disable
   - **b.** determine
   - **c.** assist
   - **d.** strike

3. exhilarate
   - **a.** help
   - **b.** cleanse
   - **c.** depress
   - **d.** frighten

4. excise
   - **a.** drop
   - **b.** inject
   - **c.** extract
   - **d.** surprise

5. eminent
   - **a.** wealthy
   - **b.** careless
   - **c.** lowly
   - **d.** famous

EXERCISE C Prefixes and Meaning

If you can learn to recognize how a prefix affects the meaning of a word, you can understand a variety of words. Choose two of the vocabulary words. On a separate sheet of paper, explain how the meaning of *e-* or *ex-* is related to the meanings of these words.

Vocabulary Power

Lesson 40 Using Test-Taking Skills
Analogies

You are likely to encounter word analogies when you take a standardized vocabulary test. This type of question asks you to look at the relationships between a word pair and then create another pair having a similar relationship. Here are some tips to help you answer these types of questions.

A. Examine carefully the relationship between the given pair of words. Decide how the words are related. For example, does one word name an action and the other word a person who completes the action? Are the words synonyms, or similar in meaning? Are they antonyms, or opposite in meaning?

B. Notice the part of speech of each word in the given pair. For example, is the pair a noun/verb combination? An adjective/adjective combination? A noun/noun combination? The pair that is the correct answer will usually represent the same parts of speech.

C. First, eliminate the answers that you are sure are wrong. For example, look for a misleading answer, different parts of speech in the given pair, or a relationship that is obviously different from the one expressed by the example pair.

D. Use your knowledge of prefixes, suffixes, and word roots to figure out the meanings of any words you don't recognize.

E. Choose the pair that is MOST like the given pair. More than one pair may seem correct. If you are confused or undecided, always refocus on the relationship between the two words in the example. Remember, you are trying to match the relationship of the given pair.

EXERCISE

Choose the letter of the word pair that best completes each analogy.

1. laugh : smile :: _____
   a. smile : joke   b. shout : mouth   c. cry : frown   d. sobbing : frowning

2. tower : height :: _____
   a. ditch : depth   b. length : width   c. truck : distance   d. building : tall

3. exactly : precisely :: _____
   a. quickly : slowly   b. quickly : rapidly   c. rudely : abrupt   d. generous : kindly

4. wind : air :: _____
   a. thunder : water   b. breath : lungs   c. heat : fireplace   d. current : water

5. wing : bird :: _____
   a. eye : face   b. cat : claw   c. fin : fish   d. arm : finger

6. hiss : snake :: _____
   a. chirp : cricket   b. thunder : storm   c. gallop : horse   d. voice : song

Vocabulary Power

Review: Unit 10

EXERCISE A

Circle the letter of the word that most clearly means the *opposite* of the boldfaced word.

1. sordid
   a. energized   b. tired   c. pure   d. thrilled

2. fidelity
   a. evil   b. health   c. brilliance   d. falseness

3. delude
   a. upset   b. comfort   c. deceive   d. guide

4. prevail
   a. criticize   b. fail   c. conquer   d. invite

5. exhilarate
   a. depress   b. energize   c. describe   d. anger

6. advocate
   a. backer   b. opponent   c. friend   d. family

7. expunge
   a. add   b. erase   c. distort   d. fight

8. arrogance
   a. speed   b. danger   c. pride   d. modesty

9. solitary
   a. alone   b. social   c. simple   d. bipolar

10. caustic
   a. severe   b. quiet   c. rude   d. gentle

EXERCISE B

Circle the word in parentheses that best completes each sentence.

1. Most people won't be impressed by a(n) (caustic, ostentatious, sordid) show of wealth and power.

2. During the violent windstorm, the boat began to (repulse, absolve, founder).

3. We don't want the decision to be based on ideas that are (kindred, disconsolate, partisan).

4. The filthiness of the old apartment building is sure to (repulse, empower, emit) potential tenants.

5. The teacher worked tirelessly to (expunge, elicit, repulse) excited responses from the tired group of students.

Vocabulary Power

Test: Unit 10

PART A

Circle the letter of the word that best completes the sentence.

1. Although the family had a great deal of money, they wanted their home to be simple and tasteful, not _____.
   a. ostentatious   **b.** sordid   **c.** solitary   **d.** evocative

2. The dean promised to _____ her of the charge that she had cheated on the test.
   a. repulse   **b.** absolve   **c.** elicit   **d.** emit

3. The play was so _____ that the actors could hear sobs rising from the audience.
   a. ostentatious   **b.** kindred   **c.** evocative   **d.** eminent

4. Renaldo was _____ for many weeks after his best friend moved across the country.
   a. sordid   **b.** disconsolate   **c.** caustic   **d.** kindred

5. In appointing a chairman, board members had to decide who had shown the greatest _____ toward the company.
   a. fidelity   **b.** exposition   **c.** expertise   **d.** solace

6. Students elected to have the _____ scholar speak at their graduation in the spring.
   a. kindred   **b.** solitary   **c.** caustic   **d.** eminent

7. The scientist looked for _____ thinkers who might back her research project with money and interest.
   a. sordid   **b.** kindred   **c.** ostentatious   **d.** solitary

8. The car began to _____ loud squealing sounds after Sal drove through the huge puddle.
   a. emit   **b.** expunge   **c.** elicit   **d.** excise

9. The _____ of the brilliant Brazilian rock climber was highly regarded.
   a. arrogance   **b.** treachery   **c.** expertise   **d.** founder

10. The race was moving along smoothly, but then runners began to _____ in the intense heat.
    a. empower   **b.** founder   **c.** excise   **d.** repulse

PART B

Choose the letter of the word or phrase that best completes each of the following sentences.

1. To be solitary is to be _____.
   a. biased   **b.** alone   **c.** unhappy   **d.** excited

2. A caustic comment is likely to _____.
   a. impress   **b.** honor   **c.** sting   **d.** bore

3. One type of exposition is _____.
   a. an election   **b.** a ballet recital   **c.** an experiment   **d.** a good friend

Vocabulary Power *continued*

4. A martyr is someone who _____.

  a. tries to impress people with wealth   **c.** tricks innocent people

  b. runs for public office   **d.** suffers for a cause

5. A partisan decision _____.

  a. protects the interests of everyone   **c.** puts personal beliefs above all else

  b. pleases only one group of people   **d.** is one that is made quickly

6. To empower someone is to _____.

  a. give authority   **c.** believe in and respect one's self

  b. recognize an unusual talent   **d.** bar someone from your home

7. An example of treachery is _____.

  a. wanting to be alone   **c.** extreme devotion to a religion

  b. cheating people who trust you   **d.** suffering for a cause

8. To prevail is to _____.

  a. fail   **b.** triumph   **c.** trick people   **d.** suffer

9. An example of a comrade is _____.

  a. a flashy home   **b.** an illness   **c.** a best friend   **d.** an extraordinary skill

10. If something begins to repulse you, you _____.

  a. try to get closer to it   **c.** decide to imitate it

  b. want to get away from it   **d.** invite other people to enjoy it

PART C

Circle the letter of the word that best completes each sentence.

1. The hawk is a fearsome _____ to its prey—the mouse.

  a. exposition   **b.** founder   **c.** predator   **d.** martyr

2. Because of her lobbying for it, she is the group's strongest _____.

  a. advocate   **b.** martyr   **c.** predator   **d.** exposition

3. What kind of reaction were you able to _____ from the trustees?

  a. prevail   **b.** repulse   **c.** emit   **d.** elicit

4. When it comes to working with computers, Jonathan wishes he had Gena's _____

  a. treachery   **b.** expertise   **c.** exposition   **d.** benefactor

5. We had to _____ a tree stump when we were clearing the field.

  a. repulse   **b.** elicit   **c.** empower   **d.** excise

Name _____ Date _____ Class _____

 Vocabulary Power

Lesson 41 Using Synonyms

What does the word **heroism** mean to you? Some people think of death-defying feats; others think of everyday actions requiring courage. All the words in this list are related somehow to heroism.

Word List

altruism	endeavor	persevere	undaunted
chivalry	intrepid	prowess	vanquish
confront	laudable		

EXERCISE A Synonyms

Each boldfaced vocabulary word below is paired with a synonym whose meaning you probably know. Brainstorm other words related to the meaning of the synonym and write your ideas on the line provided. Then, look up the vocabulary word in a dictionary and write its meaning.

1. **confront** : challenge _____

   Dictionary definition _____

2. **vanquish** : defeat _____

   Dictionary definition _____

3. **prowess** : strength _____

   Dictionary definition _____

4. **intrepid** : fearless _____

   Dictionary definition _____

5. **undaunted** : unafraid _____

   Dictionary definition _____

6. **chivalry** : nobility _____

   Dictionary definition _____

7. **altruism** : selflessness _____

   Dictionary definition _____

8. **laudable** : praiseworthy _____

   Dictionary definition _____

9. **persevere** : persist _____

   Dictionary definition _____

10. **endeavor** : effort _____

    Dictionary definition _____

Vocabulary Power *continued*

EXERCISE B True or False

Read each sentence below. Decide whether it is true or false based on the meaning of the boldfaced word. Write *true* or *false* on the line provided and briefly explain your answer.

1. An **intrepid** cyclist would probably avoid busy roads for fear of being hit by a car.

   _____

2. A warrior who had **vanquished** the enemy would be welcomed home as a hero.

   _____

3. A knight could demonstrate his **chivalry** by fleeing a battle.

   _____

4. Finding a cure for cancer would be a **laudable** achievement.

   _____

5. An animal rights activist will **persevere** in a campaign to stop animal experiments despite opposition.

   _____

EXERCISE C Multiple-Meaning Words

Several of the vocabulary words have more than one meaning. Read each sentence below and look up the definition of the boldfaced word. If the word is used correctly, write *correct*. Then, write the definition on the line provided. Otherwise, write *incorrect*.

1. Although Jennifer felt like screaming, she **vanquished** her emotions and spoke calmly.

   _____

2. Simon demonstrated his **prowess** in baseball by hitting a home run in every game.

   _____

3. The commander defeated his foes by using the medieval military strategy of **chivalry**.

   _____

4. Patrice **endeavored** to raise money for the scholarship fund by selling her hand-carved birdhouses.

   _____

5. Jono realized that the animals in the pet shop would **persevere** if they were not rescued from the fire, so he bravely rushed into the building.

   _____

Vocabulary Power

Lesson 42 The Suffixes *-ant* and *-ent*

A suffix is a word part added to the end of a word. Here's an example of how suffixes work.

Base Word

hero
("a person noted for feats of courage or nobility")

Suffix

-ic
("of or relating to")

New Word

heroic
("of or relating to a hero"; "showing the qualities of a hero")

Note that adding the suffix *-ic* changes not only the meaning of the base word **hero,** but also the part of speech from noun to adjective. The words in the list below are formed with the suffixes *-ant* and *-ent*. In these words, the suffixes mean either "being in a specified state or condition" or "a person who performs a specified action."

Word List

adherent	confidant	incessant	luxuriant
coherent	contestant	indulgent	reverent
combatant	exultant		

EXERCISE A Context Clues

Read each sentence below. Use context clues, or clues from the surrounding text, to determine the meaning of the boldfaced word. Write your definition of the word. Then, look up the word in a dictionary and write its definition.

1. This fascinating program about World War II shows the experience of the war through the eyes of one **combatant,** a French soldier.

   My definition _____

   Dictionary definition _____

2. The villain from my favorite novel has no **confidant;** he keeps all his evil secrets to himself.

   My definition _____

   Dictionary definition _____

3. The company's founder was an **adherent** of the idea that company profits should be returned to the community, so he left all his money to a community organization.

   My definition _____

   Dictionary definition _____

4. I wonder how Kevin can study with that **incessant** music playing next door.

   My definition _____

   Dictionary definition _____

Vocabulary Power *continued*

5. Her **luxuriant** black hair fell to her waist.

My definition _____

Dictionary definition _____

6. The TV biography failed to create a **coherent** picture of the rock star's life; for example, I didn't understand how other artists influenced his musical career.

My definition _____

Dictionary definition _____

7. Margie has been chosen as a **contestant** on her favorite game show; she'll have a chance to compete for fabulous prizes!

My definition _____

Dictionary definition _____

8. As the camera panned slowly over the centuries-old stained-glass windows, the narrator described the history of the church in **reverent** tones.

My definition _____

Dictionary definition _____

9. The **exultant** winners of the World Cup leaped joyfully around the field.

My definition _____

Dictionary definition _____

10. It seems rather **indulgent** to buy a second home in the country when so many people are homeless.

My definition _____

Dictionary definition _____

EXERCISE B Word Association

For each group of words, write the vocabulary word that best fits.

1. follower, believer, devotee   _____

2. unceasing, constant, persistent   _____

3. fighter, soldier, warrior   _____

4. joyful, celebrating, jubilant   _____

5. respectful, worshipful, adoring   _____

Vocabulary Power

Lesson 43 The Latin Root *scrib/script*

The Latin root *scrib* or *script*, meaning "to scratch" or "to write," is the basis for a large family of words in English. A few of these words are listed below. Look through the list for words that you know. Can you see how these words are related to the meaning of the Latin root?

Word List

inscribe	postscript	scribble	subscribe
inscription	prescribe	scripture	transcript
manuscript	proscribe		

EXERCISE A Context Clues

Read each sentence and use context clues to develop a working definition of the boldfaced vocabulary word. Write your definition of the word. Then, look up the word in a dictionary and write the definition that best fits the meaning of the sentence.

1. After hearing the author talk about her new book, I bought a copy and asked her to **inscribe** it.

   My definition _____

   Dictionary definition _____

2. Many books in the Christian Bible are also part of the Jewish sacred **scripture.**

   My definition _____

   Dictionary definition _____

3. After an unfortunate incident in the cafeteria, Ms. Jackson posted some new rules that **proscribe** throwing

   food from one table to another.

   My definition _____

   Dictionary definition _____

4. To improve your performance in school, I would **prescribe** rest, quiet, and a regular study schedule.

   My definition _____

   Dictionary definition _____

5. Peter would most likely **scribble** his term paper if his teacher did not require neatly typewritten essays.

   My definition _____

   Dictionary definition _____

6. Lee Ann marveled at the work involved in the ancient handwritten **manuscript.**

   My definition _____

   Dictionary definition _____

Vocabulary Power *continued*

7. Because the **postscript** was in different handwriting, I became suspicious.

   My definition _____

   Dictionary definition _____

8. The cost to **subscribe** to the symphony seems high, but we will enjoy all the concerts next year.

   My definition _____

   Dictionary definition _____

9. If you hear a radio program that you especially like, you can order a **transcript** and read the material yourself.

   My definition _____

   Dictionary definition _____

10. Some public buildings have an **inscription** carved into the cornerstone that gives the date of construction.

    My definition _____

    Dictionary definition _____

EXERCISE B Context Clues
Write the vocabulary word that matches each clue.

1. Computers make it easier for authors to create this. _____

2. A sacred writing is an example of this. _____

3. If you forget to say something in your letter, you can add it here. _____

4. When a community does this, it is setting a rule against something. _____

5. A doctor may do this so that you can get the medicine you need. _____

EXERCISE C Word Roots
Many other English words derive from the Latin root *scrib/script*, although their spelling may not always reveal this. Use your dictionary to solve this puzzle: All the words in the following list— except one—are derived from *scrib/script*: scribe, sculpture, shrive, circumscribe. Which one does not belong?_____

What is the root of this word, what does it mean, and what are some other English words derived from the same root?

_____

_____

_____

Vocabulary Power

Review: Unit 11

EXERCISE A

Circle the word in each set of parentheses that best completes the sentence.

1. Watching the (intrepid, incessant, indulgent) gushing of water over the falls, Melinda wondered how many gallons must flow through there each year.

2. Arnav is my closest friend and (adherent, combatant, confidant); I trust him completely and tell him all my secrets.

3. Even after losing his leg, Paul, (undaunted, laudable, luxuriant), trained for a marathon.

4. It's obvious that you should not drop chewing gum on the court, although the rules of tennis do not specifically (prescribe, proscribe, subscribe) this behavior.

5. The ideals of (chivalry, prowess, altruism) include courage, nobility, honor, and courtesy toward women.

6. The (laudable, exultant, luxuriant) trees lined the avenue.

7. Although it was nearly midnight, Sally's determination to finish the novel in time to discuss it at the book club meeting helped her to (persevere, confront, inscribe).

8. The deadline for all short-story (inscriptions, contestants, manuscripts) is the end of the month.

9. Taking a bubble bath twice a day could be considered (intrepid, laudable, indulgent).

10. It takes courage to (confront, subscribe, persevere) someone whose behavior is hurting you, but often it is the only way to make the person realize the effects of his or her actions.

EXERCISE B

For each boldfaced word, circle the letter of the word that has most nearly the same meaning.

1. vanquish
   a. disappear   b. surrender   c. flee   d. conquer

2. altruism
   a. courage   b. selflessness   c. determination   d. sadness

3. incessant
   a. constant   b. pleasing   c. cruel   d. occasional

4. proscribe
   a. embrace   b. medicate   c. forbid   d. erase

5. laudable
   a. foolish   b. commendable   c. brave   d. loud

Vocabulary Power

Test: Unit 11

PART A

Circle the letter of the word that best completes each sentence.

1. Key ingredients of a good television game show include a host with an appealing personality, a game that is easy to understand, and at least one enthusiastic _____.
   a. adherent   **b.** contestant   **c.** confidant   **d.** combatant

2. Most worthwhile goals require you to _____ despite obstacles.
   a. vanquish   **b.** confront   **c.** proscribe   **d.** persevere

3. Building the pyramids in ancient Egypt was a(n) _____ that required brilliant engineering and the labor of millions of slaves.
   a. altruism   **b.** scripture   **c.** endeavor   **d.** inscription

4. The costs to _____ to the club far outweigh any benefits we might receive.
   a. prescribe   **b.** persevere   **c.** subscribe   **d.** confront

5. Geena's letter contained at least one _____ too many; she might as well have written a second letter!
   a. manuscript   **b.** postscript   **c.** transcript   **d.** adherent

6. Despite the thin air and frigid wind near the top of Mount Everest, the climbers remained _____ as they began the last and most treacherous part of their journey.
   a. coherent   **b.** indulgent   **c.** reverent   **d.** undaunted

7. The _____ gale-force winds caused the ship to founder.
   a. incessant   **b.** luxuriant   **c.** intrepid   **d.** exultant

8. The principal mailed a(n) _____ of the student's grades to her new high school.
   a. transcript   **b.** manuscript   **c.** inscription   **d.** postscript

9. The noisy children were warned to show a more _____ attitude at temple.
   a. intrepid   **b.** reverent   **c.** coherent   **d.** exultant

10. Angelo's speech was _____; all his examples clearly supported his main idea.
   a. undaunted   **b.** coherent   **c.** incessant   **d.** indulgent

PART B

Circle the letter of the item that best completes each sentence.

1. The scriptures of a religious faith are important because _____.
   a. they provide a place where the faithful can gather to worship
   b. they are the sacred writings on which the faith is based
   c. they contain a current listing of the people in the community
   d. they are the leaders to whom others in the community look for guidance

Vocabulary Power

Vocabulary Power *continued*

2. A landscape described as luxuriant would probably look _____.
   a. brown and withered, with few plants or animals
   b. cold and windswept, with a dazzling cover of bright white snow
   c. crowded with people, cars, and many shops and restaurants
   d. green and moist, bursting with healthy vegetation

3. An example of prowess is _____.
   a. winning a professional golf tournament
   b. having the courage to enter a writing contest even though you are unlikely to win
   c. letting your little sister beat you at checkers
   d. winning the lottery

4. One way to vanquish your fear of something is to _____.
   a. avoid situations that make you feel afraid
   b. never tell anyone you have felt afraid
   c. face the thing that frightens you until you are no longer afraid of it
   d. try to make others feel afraid of that thing too

5. You might call a child intrepid if she _____.
   a. hides behind her parents whenever strangers enter the room
   b. spends most of her time alone in her room with her stuffed animals
   c. bites her fingernails when she feels afraid of something
   d. faces new experiences bravely

PART C

Analogies show relationships between things or ideas. For example, in the analogy *drop* : *break* :: *ignite* : *burn*, the relationship in each pair is "cause to effect." If you drop something, you cause it to break; if you ignite something, you cause it to burn. Complete each analogy by determining the relationship between the first pair of words. Then, choose the letter of the word that creates the same relationship in the second pair.

1. undaunted : fearful :: coherent : _____
   a. sensible   b. whole   c. inconsistent   d. sloppy

2. combatant : fight :: adherent : _____
   a. talk   b. believe   c. reject   d. rejoice

3. chivalry : honor :: altruism : _____
   a. stubbornness   b. self-sacrifice c. ignorance   d. sweetness

4. sketch : painting :: manuscript : _____
   a. gravestone   b. sculpture   c. letter   d. book

5. argument : coherent :: confidant : _____
   a. trustworthy   b. sneaky   c. kind   d. fair

Vocabulary Power

Lesson 44 Using Context Clues

"What's so funny?" is a very personal question. Your sense of humor is as unique as your fingerprints. It's fun to share a laugh with a friend or even with a complete stranger. Laughter brings people together. The words in this list all have something to do with comic perspectives.

Word List

droll	jocular	slapstick	whimsical
facetious	parody	wag	witticism
farcical	satire		

EXERCISE A Context Clues

Read each sentence below and use context clues to determine the meaning of the boldfaced word. Write your definition of the word. Then, look up the word in a dictionary and write its definition.

1. The story I read to my little brother last night featured a **droll** elf whose strange behavior made us laugh.

   My definition _____

   Dictionary definition _____

2. Joanne enjoyed the play because she likes **farcical** humor, but the plot was too far-fetched and the characters too exaggerated for my taste.

   My definition _____

   Dictionary definition _____

3. The Three Stooges were masters of **slapstick** humor; they were forever tripping over things, chasing one another around the room, or hitting one another over the head.

   My definition _____

   Dictionary definition _____

4. At first, I thought Dad was disappointed with the clay pot I'd made for him in art class, but the twinkle in his eye made me realize that his remark was **facetious**.

   My definition _____

   Dictionary definition _____

5. A well-known **witticism** of Mark Twain is, "It is better to keep your mouth shut and appear stupid than to open it and remove all doubt."

   My definition _____

   Dictionary definition _____

Vocabulary Power continued

6. In his **satire**, *Gulliver's Travels*, Jonathan Swift creates the inhabitants of four imaginary nations to criticize human pride, greed, selfishness, and dishonesty.

My definition _____

Dictionary definition _____

7. Robert's performance will be a **parody** of a political speech; he will discuss several fictitious issues, using the language and hand gestures of a politician.

My definition _____

Dictionary definition _____

8. Myra's **jocular** Uncle Fred loves to clown around by pretending to pull coins from the ears of her little sisters.

My definition _____

Dictionary definition _____

9. Stella's a real **wag** and can liven up any party with her jokes.

My definition _____

Dictionary definition _____

10. Writers of fantasy books must have very **whimsical** imaginations; their characters revel in the unexpected.

My definition _____

Dictionary definition _____

EXERCISE B Analogies

Analogies show relationships between things or ideas. For example, in the analogy *soldier : fight ::* *chef : cook,* **the relationship in each pair is "actor to action." (A soldier fights; a chef cooks). Complete each analogy below by determining the relationship between the first pair of words. Then, circle the letter of the word that creates the same relationship in the second pair.**

1. facetious : serious :: whimsical : _____
   a. predictable   **b.** funny   **c.** old   **d.** brave

2. storyteller : tale :: wag : _____
   a. song   **b.** dog   **c.** joke   **d.** lie

3. puzzle : confusion :: witticism : _____
   a. disdain   **b.** criticism   **c.** surprise   **d.** humor

4. whimsy : whimsical :: farce : _____
   a. facetious   **b.** parodoxical   **c.** farcical   **d.** jocular

Vocabulary Power

Lesson 45 The Prefixes *sym-* and *syn-*

A prefix is a word part that appears at the beginning of a word. Because a prefix has its own meaning, it changes the meaning of the base word or root to which it is added. For example, the Greek prefix *sym-*, which can also be spelled *syn-*, can mean "together," "with," "same," or "similar." Study the words in the list below, all of which have the prefix *sym-* or *syn-*. Do you know any of these words? If so, can you see how their meanings are related to the meaning of the prefix?

Word List			
symbiotic	**syndicate**	**synonymous**	**syntax**
symmetrical	**syndrome**	**synopsis**	**synthesis**
sympathetic	**synergy**		

EXERCISE A Context Clues

For each sentence below, use context clues to determine the meaning of the boldfaced vocabulary word. Write your definition of the word. Then, look up the word in a dictionary and write its definition.

1. The heads of several companies formed a **syndicate** to bring a new stadium to the city.

   My definition _____

   Dictionary definition _____

2. Some **symbiotic** relationships involve two species that benefit each other; for example, a bee takes pollen from one flower and pollinates another.

   My definition _____

   Dictionary definition _____

3. Most writing follows standard rules of **syntax**; that is, word arrangement.

   My definition _____

   Dictionary definition _____

4. Recycled plastic is a **synthesis** of several kinds of plastic combined to form a new product.

   My definition _____

   Dictionary definition _____

5. The wings on the child's homemade angel costume were not **symmetrical**—one wing was larger than the other.

   My definition _____

   Dictionary definition _____

6. Symptoms including depression, feelings of guilt, flashbacks to combat experiences, and sensitivity to loud noises are part of a **syndrome** known as post-traumatic stress disorder that afflicts many war veterans.

   My definition _____

   Dictionary definition _____

7. Every time she thought about her friend's broken ankle, Karen experienced **sympathetic** pain in her own ankle.

My definition _____

Dictionary definition _____

8. When the two companies began working together, their **synergy** helped them double their profits.

My definition _____

Dictionary definition _____

9. Do you know if "quip" is **synonymous** with "witticism," or do the two words have slightly different meanings?

My definition _____

Dictionary definition _____

10. Jason's book report was so vague that his teacher wondered if he had read only a **synopsis**.

My definition _____

Dictionary definition _____

EXERCISE B **Multiple-Meaning Words**

Many words have more than one meaning. Each meaning, however, is based on the meaning of the root word. The word *sympathetic*, for example, has the Greek root *pathos*, meaning "feeling." A dictionary entry for *sympathetic* lists several different meanings, but all of them are related to the root meaning. Use a dictionary to help you write the precise definition of *sympathy* as it is used in each sentence below.

1. She made a **sympathetic** gesture toward the sick child.

_____

2. The lab students observed the reaction of the frog's **sympathetic** nervous system.

_____

3. When the violinist plucked the major chords, certain minor chords sounded by **sympathetic** vibration.

_____

4. Various health organizations banded together in a **sympathetic** association.

_____

EXERCISE C **Word Roots**

You already know that *syn-* means "together" or "with." Can you explain how the meaning of this prefix relates to the meaning of the word *synopsis*? Use a dictionary to research the origin of *synopsis*. What is its root, and from what language is this root? Use the back of this sheet to answer these questions.

Vocabulary Power

Lesson 46 The Root *spec*

The Latin root *spec*, meaning "to look at," is the basis for a large family of words in English. Think of all the different ways we use the idea of looking. For example, you can view something with your eyes or examine it with your mind. You can look up to someone or down on someone. The words in the list below all come from the root *spec*.

Word List

conspicuous	introspection	prospective	specter
despicable	perspective	retrospective	speculate
espionage	perspicacious		

EXERCISE A Synonyms

Each boldfaced word below is paired with a synonym whose meaning you probably know. Brainstorm other words related to the meaning of the synonym and write your ideas on the line provided. Then, look up the vocabulary word in a dictionary and write its meaning.

1. **perspective** : outlook _____

   Dictionary definition _____

2. **speculate** : reflect _____

   Dictionary definition _____

3. **specter** : ghost _____

   Dictionary definition _____

4. **perspicacious** : shrewd _____

   Dictionary definition _____

5. **espionage** : spying _____

   Dictionary definition _____

6. **prospective** : likely _____

   Dictionary definition _____

7. **conspicuous** : obvious _____

   Dictionary definition _____

8. **introspection** : self-examination _____

   Dictionary definition _____

9. **retrospective** : remembering _____

   Dictionary definition _____

Vocabulary Power continued

10. **despicable** : hateful _____

Dictionary definition _____

EXERCISE B Usage

Read each sentence and decide whether it is true or false based on the meaning of the boldfaced word. Write *true* or *false* on the line provided and briefly explain your answer.

1. A **perspicacious** person is likely to overlook things that are obvious to other people.

_____

2. A person who engages in **introspection** probably has a deep understanding of his or her own feelings.

_____

3. If you are trying to blend in with a crowd of people, you should wear **conspicuous** clothing.

_____

4. A weather forecast is a **retrospective** look at what the weather might be in the coming days and weeks.

_____

EXERCISE C Usage

Circle the letter of the word that best completes each sentence.

1. A person who was caught stealing secrets from one company and giving the information to another company would be accused of industrial _____.
   a. introspection   b. specter   c. perspective   d. espionage

2. We expect to interview all _____ candidates by Friday.
   a. conspicuous   b. prospective   c. despicable   d. perspicacious

3. A career choice is difficult for many young people, but some degree of _____ can help them.
   a. espionage   b. perspective   c. introspection   d. specter

4. Stefan worried that the coffee stain on his tie was _____, but no one else even noticed it.
   a. conspicuous   b. perspicacious   c. retrospective   d. prospective

5. If you find reptiles _____, a career in herpetology, the study of reptiles, is not the best choice for you.
   a. prospective   b. despicable   c. perspicacious   d. retrospective

EXERCISE D Multiple-Meaning Word

You have already learned what the word *retrospective* means when it is used as an adjective. Use your dictionary to find out what it means when used as a noun and write the definition here.

_____

_____

Vocabulary Power

Review: Unit 12

EXERCISE

Circle the letter of the word that best completes each sentence.

1. The play was successful because of the excellent _____ among the director, cast, and crew, whose talents all complemented each other.
   a. parody   **b.** synergy   **c.** introspection   **d.** synopsis

2. Not all _____ relationships benefit both organisms; for example, a tapeworm lives inside its host and actually harms the host.
   a. symbiotic   **b.** jocular   **c.** despicable   **d.** synonymous

3. I like Woody Allen's _____, "I don't want to achieve immortality through my work. I want to achieve immortality by not dying."
   a. syntax   **b.** witticism   **c.** parody   **d.** wag

4. Most people's faces are not perfectly _____; the right side is slightly different from the left.
   a. synonymous   **b.** symmetrical   **c.** sympathetic   **d.** symbiotic

5. When you first start studying German, you may find the _____ difficult because the various parts of a sentence don't appear in the order you expect.
   a. satire   **b.** specter   **c.** syndrome   **d.** syntax

6. The exhibit was a _____ of paintings the artist had created during the first forty years of her career.
   a. retrospective   **b.** satire   **c.** syndicate   **d.** perspective

7. This disease is a(n) _____ marked by the simultaneous occurrence of several symptoms.
   a. parody   **b.** introspection   **c.** syndrome   **d.** espionage

8. I've never read *Wuthering Heights,* so I need a brief _____ of the plot.
   a. wag   **b.** synopsis   **c.** witticism   **d.** syndicate

9. A political _____ would point out the human weaknesses displayed by ambitious politicians.
   a. perspective   **b.** synthesis   **c.** espionage   **d.** satire

10. At first Sharon could not tell whether Roderick's remark was serious or _____.
    a. synonymous   **b.** conspicuous   **c.** retrospective   **d.** facetious

11. The movie had both witty dialogue and _____ comedy, including a scene in which a clumsy waiter dumps a tray of food into the lap of the beautiful heiress.
    a. jocular   **b.** slapstick   **c.** despicable   **d.** perspicacious

12. Reading a good novel can give you a new _____ because it allows you to see things through the eyes of a character whose life may be very different from your own.
    a. synergy   **b.** introspection   **c.** perspective   **d.** specter

Vocabulary Power

Test: Unit 12

PART A

Circle the word in each set of parentheses that best completes the sentence.

1. My Latin teacher always complains about my (syndicate, synergy, syntax); I use the correct words but place them in the wrong order.

2. At a somber event such as a funeral, you would probably hear very few (perspicacious, sympathetic, facetious) comments.

3. (Introspection, Espionage, Satire) often involves the theft of military secrets by one government from another.

4. Steve can do a good (parody, witticism, wag) of student council meetings because he is able to imitate the speech and mannerisms of each person involved.

5. In the ghost story I'm reading, some of the (wags, specters, perspectives) are friendly and others are scary.

6. Juliet didn't want to agree to the proposed plan until she'd had time to consider all the (symbiotic, farcical, prospective) consequences.

7. This fast-food restaurant wants to make its name (synonymous, perspicacious, facetious) with great French fries, so that whenever someone thinks of fries, they think of the restaurant.

8. Jill's poem is a perfect (syndrome, retrospective, synthesis) of vivid imagery, clever insights, and pleasing rhythm.

9. From my (specter, synopsis, perspective), teens want more intelligent films.

10. In the new millennium, many publications are taking a (conspicuous, perspicacious, retrospective) look at the past century.

11. My story is a (synthesis, parody, satire); it tries to subtly portray such human flaws as envy, greed, and cruelty.

12. The outstanding (syntax, synergy, synopsis) between the athletes and their coach led to a winning season.

13. Lila is a (perspicacious, conspicuous, prospective) observer who notices everything that happens around her.

14. A good (parody, synopsis, wag) should outline the major events of a story but omit less important details.

15. Through (introspection, espionage, retrospective), you can explore your own deepest beliefs and feelings.

PART B

For each boldfaced vocabulary word, circle the word that is most nearly *opposite* in meaning.

1. conspicuous
   - a. bright
   - b. clear
   - c. sad
   - d. subtle

2. despicable
   - a. praiseworthy
   - b. disgusting
   - c. soft
   - d. funny

Vocabulary Power *continued*

3. droll
   a. happy   **b.** somber   **c.** foolish   **d.** generous

4. symmetrical
   a. ugly   **b.** unbalanced   **c.** circular   **d.** incomprehensible

5. jocular
   a. serious   **b.** uplifting   **c.** distasteful   **d.** cruel

6. whimsical
   a. fantastic   **b.** silly   **c.** predictable   **d.** admirable

7. symbiotic
   a. predatory   **b.** unrelated   **c.** growing   **d.** hungry

8. retrospective
   a. inclusive   **b.** critical   **c.** celebratory   **d.** forward-looking

PART C

Circle the best answer to each question.

1. What is an example of a syndicate?
   a. two high-school students who take all the same classes
   b. a word that has nearly the same meaning as another word
   c. a play with a ridiculous plot and outrageous characters
   d. several organizations working together to block plans to cut down a forest

2. Which scene would you be most likely to see in a slapstick comedy?
   a. a character slips on a banana peel
   b. two characters sit in a kitchen and make light conversation
   c. a comedian stands in front of a microphone and tells jokes
   d. a character from a big city does not understand the social customs of a small town

abhor   ab hôr´

absolve   ab zolv´

abyss   ə bis´

accentuate   ak sen´chōō āt´

accolades   ak´ə lādz´

adept   ə dept´

adequate   ad´ə kwət

adherent   ad hēr´ənt

advocate   ad´və kāt´

aesthetic   es thet´ik

affront   ə frunt´

agenda   ə jen´də

alluring   ə loor´ing

altruism   al´trōō iz´ əm

anachronism   ə nak´rə niz´əm

anecdote   an´ik dōt´

animated   an´ə mā´tid

anonymous   ə non´ə məs

anthropomorphic   an´thrə pə môr´fik

antibiotic   an´tē bī ot´ik

antidote   an´ti dōt´

antipathy   an tip´ə thē

antithesis   an tith´ə sis

antonym   an´tə nim´

apprehend   ap´ri hend´

arboretum   är´bə rē´təm

arrogance   ar´ə gəns

average   av´rij

axiom   ak´sē əm

backlash   bak´lash´

balmy   bä´mē

beguile   bi gīl´

bench mark   bench´märk

benefactor   ben´ə fak´tər

benign   bi nīn´

bicuspid   bī kus´pid

biennial   bī en´ē al

bigamy   big´ə mē

bilateral   bī lat´ər əl

bilingual   bī ling´gwəl

blitz   blits

bow   bō (n. or v.), bou (n. or v.)

brink   bringk

calf   kaf

candor   kan´dər

cataclysm   kat´ə kliz´əm

caustic   kôs´tik

centralize   sen´trə līz´

chivalry   shiv´əl rē

chronic   kron´ik

chronicle   kron´i kəl

chronograph   kron´ə graf´

chronological   kron´ə loj´ i kəl

chronology   krə nol´ə jē

circumlocution   sur´kəm lō kū´shən

circumstance   sur´kəm stans´

cognition   kog nish´ən

coherent   kō hēr´ənt

combatant   kəm bat´ənt

common sense   kom´ən sens

complement   kom´plə mənt

comrade   kom´rad

condescend   kon´di send´

confidant   kon´fə dant´

confound   kən found´

confront   kən frunt´

conscientiously   kon´shē en´shəs lē

console   kon´sōl

conspicuous   kən spik´ū əs

constrain   kən strān´

constrict   kən strikt´

contestant   kən tes´tənt

contraband   kon´trə band´

contradictory   kon´trə dik´tər ē

converge   kən vurj´

convoluted   kon´və lōō´tid

corpulent   kôr´pyə lənt

counterweight   koun´tər wāt´

cumulative   kū´myə lə tiv

curtail   kər tāl´

dauntless   dônt´lis

defray   di frā´

dehydration   dē´hī drā´shən

delectable   di lek´tə bəl

delude   di lōōd´

delve   delv

demure   di myoor´

denomination   di nom´ə nā´shən

despicable   des´pi kə bəl

destitute   des´tə tōōt´

diction dik′shən

digression di gresh′ən

diligent dil′ə jənt

disconsolate dis kon′sə lit

disdain dis dān′

disillusion dis′i lōō′zhən

dispassionate dis pash′ə nit

disperse dis purs′

disposed dis pōzd′

disposition dis′pə zish′ən

distress dis tres′

dormant dôr′mənt

droll drōl

dynamic dī nam′ik

eccentric ik sen′trik

economize i kon′ə mīz′

ecstatic ek stat′ik

elaborate i lab′ər it (adj.), i lab′ə rāt′ (v.)

elated i lā′tid

elegy el′ə jē

elicit i lis′it

emboldened em bōld′ənd

eminent em′ə nənt

emit i mit′

empower em pou′ər

endeavor en dev′ər

endorse en dôrs′

enhance en hans′

ensemble än säm′bəl

ephemeral i fem′ər əl

epitaph ep′ə taf′

epithet ep′ə thet′

equalize ēk′wə līz′

equanimity ēk′wə nim′ə tē

equilibrium ēk′wə lib′rē əm

equivocal i kwiv′ə kəl

espionage es′pē ə näzh′

esteem es tēm′

euthanasia ū′thə nā′zhə

evade i vād′

evocative i vok′ə tiv

excise ek′sīz (n.), ek sīz′ (v.)

exhilarate ig zil′ə rāt′

expend iks pend′

expertise ek′spər tēz′

exposition eks′pə zish′ən

expunge iks punj′

exultant ig zult′ənt

facetious fə sē′shəs

farcical fär′si kəl

fidelity fi del′ə tē

flaunt flônt

formidable fôr′mi də bəl

fortitude fôr′tə tōōd′

fortuitous fôr′tōō′ə təs

founder foun′dər

fractional frak′shən əl

fractious frak′shəs

fragment frag′mənt

frail frāl

fraught frôt

fret fret

fritter frit′ər

frivolous friv′ə ləs

gaudy gô′dē

genealogy jē′nē ol′ə jē

giddy gid′ē

grapple grap′əl

gratify grat′ə fī′

gridlock grid′lok

grotesque grō tesk′

hidebound hīd′bound′

hierarchy hī′ə rär′kē

hold hōld

homonym hom′ə nim′

hop hop

hypodermic hī′pə dur′mik

idealize ī dē′ə līz′

ideology ī′dē ol′ə jē

ignominy ig′nə min′ē

immobilize i mō′bə līz′

impede im pēd′

impetuous im pech′ōō əs

impressionable im presh′ə nə bəl

incessant in ses′ənt

indulgent in dul′jənt

infamous in′fə məs

infraction in frak′shən

infringe in frinj′

innocuous i nok′ū əs

innovate in′ə vāt′

inscribe in skrīb′

inscription in skrip′shən

inscrutable in skrōō′tə bəl

insinuation in sin′ū ā′shən

insoluble in sol′yə bəl

insuperable in sōō′pər ə bəl

interact in′tə rakt′

intercom in′tər kom′

interject in′tər jekt′

interlaced in′tər lāst′

intermediary in′tər mē′dē er′ē

interminable in tur′mi nə bəl

intermittent in′tər mit′ənt

interplay in′tər plā′

interrogate in ter′ə gāt′

interrogation in ter′ə gā′shən

intersperse in′tər spurs′

intervention in′tər ven′chən

intramural in′trə myoor′əl

intrastate in′trə stāt′

intravenous in′trə vē′nəs

intrepid in trep′id

introspection in′trə spek′shən

invincible in vin′sə bəl

jocular jok′yə lər

kindred kin′drid

kowtow kou′tou′

lap lap

laud lôd

laudable lô′də bəl

luxuriant lug zhoor′ē ənt

malicious mə lish′əs

manipulate mə nip′yə lāt′

manuscript man′yə skript′

martyr mär′tər

materialize mə tēr′ē ə līz′

maximize mak′sə mīz′

mediocre mē′dē ō′kər

medley med′lē

mesmerize mez′mə rīz′

microbe mī′krōb

microbiology mī′krō bī ol′ə jē

microfilm mī′krə film′

microscopic mī′krə skop′ik

midcontinent mid′kont′ən ənt

midlife mid′līf

misnomer mis nō′mər

momentum mō men′təm

monogamy mə nog′ə mē

monolith mon′ə lith′

monologue mon′ə lôg′

monotheism mon′ə thē iz′əm

monotony mə not′ən ē

mundane mun dān′

muted mūt′id

nadir nā′dər

naive nä ēv′

narrate nar′āt

nautical nô′ti kəl

nomenclature nō′mən klā′chər

nominal nom′ən əl

nonchalant non′shə länt′

obliterate ə blit′e rāt′

obnoxious ob nok′shəs

obscurity əb skyoor′ə tē

obstruct əb strukt′

obtrude əb trōōd′

obtuse əb tōōs′

oppugn ə pyūn′

opulent op′yə lənt

osprey os′prē

ostentatious os′tən tā′shəs

outsource out′sôrs′

overkill ō′vər kil′

pall pôl

pallid pal′id

palpable pal′pə bəl

panoramic pan′ə ram′ik

parody par′ə dē

partisan pär′tə zən

passive pas′iv

patronize pā′trə nīz′

pensive pen′siv

perception pər sep′shən

periphery pə rif′ər ē

permeate pur′mē āt′

perseverance pur′sə vēr′əns

persevere pur′sə vēr′

perspective pər spek′tiv

perspicacious pur´spə kā´shəs

pervade pər vād´

pestilent pes´tə lənt

picturesque pik´chə resk´

pleased plēzd

poignant poin´yənt

postscript pōst´skript´

precipitous pri sip´ə təs

predator pred´ə tər

predecessors pred´ə ses´ərs

prescribe pri skrīb´

prestige pres tēzh´

pretentious pri ten´shəs

prevail pri vāl´

prodigy prod´ə jē

progeny proj´ə nē

proponent prə pō´nənt

proscribe prō skrīb´

prospective prə spek´tiv

protracted prō trakt´id

prowess prou´is

pseudonym sōō´də nim´

psychopath sī´kə path´

rationalize rash´ən əl īz´

recourse rē´kôrs´

recuperate ri kōō´pə rāt´

refractory ri frak´tər ē

refute ri fūt´

regress ri gres´

rejuvenated ri jōō´və nāt´id

remorse ri môrs´

renown ri noun´

renowned ri nound´

repel ri pel´

reprehend rep´ri hend´

repulse ri puls´

resentment ri zent´mənt

resigned ri zīnd´

resilient ri zil´yənt

resplendent ri splen´dənt

restraint ri strānt´

retort ri tôrt´

retract ri trakt´

retrospective ret´rə spek´tiv

revel rev´əl

reverent rev´ər ənt

reverie rev´ər ē

rift rift

sagacious sə gā´shəs

satire sat´īr

scribble skrib´əl

scripture skrip´chər

scrutinize skrōōt´ən īz´

sedate si dāt´

sentiment sen´tə mənt

serendipity ser´ən dip´ə tē

slapstick slap´stik´

solace sol´is

solitary sol´ə ter´ē

solitude sol´ə tōōd´

sonorous sə nôr´əs

sordid sôr´did

sparse spärs

specter spek´tər

speculate spek´yə lāt´

stagnation stag´nā shən

stalwart stôl´wərt

straits strāts

stress stres

stricture strik´chər

stringent strin´jənt

stupor stōō´pər

suave swäv

subconscious sub kon´shəs

submerge səb murj´

subscribe səb skrīb´

substandard sub stan´dərd

subtle sut´əl

superhighway sōō´pər hī´wā´

superlative sə pur´lə tiv

suppress sə pres´

symbiotic sim´bī ot´ik

symmetrical si met´ri kəl

sympathetic sim´pə thet´ik

synchronicity sing´krə ni´sə tē

synchronize sing´krə nīz´

syndicate sin´di kit

syndrome sin´drōm´

synergy sin´ər jē

synonymous si non´ə məs

synopsis   si nop′sis
syntax   sin′taks
synthesis   sin′thə sis
systematic   sis′tə mat′ik
tantalize   tant′əl īz′
temperate   tem′pər it
tentative   ten′tə tiv
tip-off   tip′ôf′
torrid   tôr′id
torsion   tôr′shən
traction   trak′shən
transcribe   tran skrīb′
transcript   tran′skript′
transient   tran′shənt
traumatic   trô mat′ik
treachery   treach′ər ē
tribulation   trib′yə lā′shən
tumult   tōō′məlt
ultimate   ul′tə mit
undaunted   un dôn′tid
underdog   un′dər dôg′
unerring   un ur′ing
unify   ū′nə fī′
unrequited   un′ri kwī′tid
unrestrained   un′ri strānd′
vanquish   vang′kwish
vigilant   vij′ə lənt
virtuoso   vur′chōō ō′sō
vivacious   vi vā′shəs
volatile   vol′ə til
voracious   vô rā′shəs
wag   wag
wan   won
wanton   wont′ən
wary   wār′ē
wend   wend
whet   hwet
whimsical   hwim′zi kəl
wind chime   wind′chīm
witticism   wit′i siz′əm
zealously   zel′əs lē
zenith   zē′nith

Unit 1

Lesson 1

A. Accept any words and situations that relate directly or indirectly to the vocabulary word
1. steep; extremely steep
2. elusive; delicate, difficult to detect
3. muffled; toned down, softened
4. passionately; sincerely, enthusiastically
5. remove; totally erase or destroy
6. efficiently; dutifully, carefully, following good moral conduct
7. time line; arrangement of events in time
8. spread; diffuse
9. edge; edge of a cliff; beginning point
10. scatter; scatter in different directions

B. 1. precipitous 2. subtle 3. chronology
4. muted 5. obliterate 6. disperse
7. conscientiously 8. zealously 9. permeate
10. brink

C. 1. zealously 2. permeate
3. conscientiously 4. disperse

Lesson 2

A. 1. volleyball teams at school, wall of an organ
2. telephone, walkie-talkie, speakers
3. serious commentary and humor, a hot drink and spices
4. teasing conversation, boxing, counterpoint
5. school debating competition
6. jump in with a comment in a discussion
7. messenger between two groups, mediator, solving a conflict between two people
8. question crime suspects, witnesses at trials
9. rain showers, static on a radio
10. shots given in a hospital, veins, blood flow

B. 1. intermittent 2. correct 3. intercom
4. correct 5. correct

C. 1. interplay 2. interlace 3. intramural
4. interrogate 5. intermediary 6. intermittent
7. intravenous 8. interject 9. intrastate
10. intercom

Lesson 3

A. Sample dictionary definitions are provided.
1. passion; unaffected by strong personal emotions; fair
2. fame; having a bad reputation; disgraceful
3. system; according to a system; thorough and regular
4. dispose; usual emotional response; manner

B. 1. retort: answer in a quick or biting manner; torsion: twisting or turning
2. regress: move backward; return to a previous, usually worse, state; digression: turning away from the main subject when speaking or writing
3. traction: act of drawing or pulling; pulling power; protracted: drawn out in time

C. 1. No. They would spin or sink down and not be able to pull the car forward.
2. Yes, if the joke wanders far from the main topic.
3. Yes. He was responsible for the killing of millions of innocent people.
4. Probably not. He would likely be influenced by positive feelings for the skater who is his daughter or son.
5. Yes. He or she would be organized and thorough.

D. 1. regress 2. infamous 3. traction
4. systematic 5. retort

Lesson 4

A. 1. place where many different trees, shrubs, and other plants are grown for scientific and educational purposes.
2. relating to ships, sailors, or navigation on water
3. or series
4. choice and use of words
5. difficult to interpret
6. an unbroken view of the entire area
7. come together
8. delightful
9. lower oneself to a level considered beneath one's dignity
10. poem or song expressing sorrow for the dead.

B. Sentences should include a clear definition of the word.
1. not easily understood, mysterious
2. very pleasing, especially to the taste

Review: Unit 1

A. 1. intermittent 2. disposition
3. muted 4. intermediary
5. regress 6. disperse
7. interject 8. chronology
9. zealously 10. precipitous

B. Accept any answer that shows a clear understanding of the phrase. Sample answers are provided.
1. a football game between two schools in Utah
2. beige
3. specific steps followed when recording a greeting on an answering machine
4. a door that sticks on humid days
5. a list of competition dates leading to the state marching band finals starting with the earliest date
6. your response when someone makes a sarcastic remark.

Test: Unit 1

A. 1. a 2. b 3. b
4. d 5. b 6. b
7. d 8. c 9. c
10. b

B. 1. a 2. a 3. c
4. c 5. b 6. c
7. d 8. d 9. b
10. a 11. b 12. a
13. c 14. d 15. c

Unit 2

Lesson 5

A. Sample synonyms and dictionary definitions are provided.
1. causing dizziness. giddy: lighthearted; silly; foolish
2. a boring speech. interminable: having or seeming to have no end.
3. feeling while walking on a dark street. wary: watchful, cautious
4. a long story with many characters and subplots. convoluted: having many overlapping folds or paths; complicated
5. pretending to be busy to get out of doing chores. evade: escape or avoid by cleverness
6. a rubber knife. innocuous: harmless
7. planting flowers in front of a building; make greater in value or beauty. enhance: heighten; intensify
8. a thorny hedge you can't step or climb over. insuperable: impossible to overcome
9. film star promotes a product. endorse: give approval or support to
10. car travel slowed by a blizzard. impede: interfere with; slow the progress of

B. 1. convoluted 2. impede 3. giddy
4. innocuous 5. interminable 6. insuperable
7. enhance 8. endorse 9. evade
10. wary

Lesson 6

A. Sample dictionary definitions are provided. Accept sentences that show a clear understanding of the word's meaning.
1. rejuvenated: made youthful or new again
2. repel: to keep away; fight back
3. refute: to prove false by argument

4. retract: to take back; draw back

5. resigned: deliberately giving up; accepting

6. resentment: ill will felt as a result of a perceived insult or injury

7. recuperate: to recover health or strength

8. recourse: turning too someone or something for help or protection

9. renowned: widely honored or famous

10. remorse: deep pain caused by guilt for past wrongdoing

B. 1. resigned   2. rejuvenated

    3. recourse   4. repel

C. 1. recuperate   2. remorse   3. resentment

    4. repel   5. rejuvenated   6. resigned

Lesson 7

A. Sample answers are provided

1. Become equal. Make equal.

2. Become central. Draw toward a center; bring under central control.

3. Become ideal or perfect. To regard as excellent or perfect.

4. Cause to become the greatest. Increase or make as great as possible.

5. Become careful in spending money. Reduce spending or avoid waste.

6. Make unable to move. Make unmovable or fix the position of.

7. Treat with close examination. Examine or observe carefully.

8. Become substantial or real. Take on concrete form; appear suddenly.

9. Treat with hypnotism. Hypnotize; fascinate.

10. Treat with reason; make something understandable. To come up with believable but untrue reasons for one's behavior.

B. Answers will vary. Accept all explanations that show a clear understanding of the word's meaning.

1. Yes; their monotonous sound and movement could hypnotize you.

2. No; but a magician might make an elephant seem to appear suddenly.

3. Yes; the person often thinks the loved one is perfect.

4. Yes; walking would save resources.

5. Yes; he or she would be making up an untrue reason for their actions or feelings.

6. Yes; you should study it critically.

7. No; millions of tickets are typically sold, so buying three would not significantly increase your chance of winning.

8. Yes; In A.D. 79, Pompeii was destroyed and the surrounding towns were immobilized by the eruption of Vesuvius.

Lesson 8

1. ensemble. It comes from the Latin word *insimul*, which means "at the same time." In an ensemble, a group of people or things together at the same time create one effect.

2. blitzkrieg. It literally means "lightning war," or a sudden, swift military attack.

3. An intense campaign or a bombardment of ads. Ads for the candidate might be placed simultaneously in newspapers and magazines and on radio and television over a short period of time.

4. *kou* means "knock" and *tou* means "head." A person who kowtows touches, or knocks, his or her forehead to the ground. Adopting this body posture before someone suggests subservience, worship, or extreme respect; therefore, to kowtow is to treat someone with extreme, servant-like respect.

5. Path high over the head.

Review: Unit 2

1. a   2. d   3. d

4. b   5. c   6. a

7. b   8. c   9. a

10. d

Test: Unit 2

A. 1. d   2. b   3. a

    4. c   5. b   6. c

    7. b   8. b   9. d

    10. a   11. b   12. c

B. 1. c   2. a   3. d

4. a   5. b   6. b

7. b   8. c

Unit 3

Lesson 9

A. Sample synonyms and dictionary definitions are provided.

1. fatal, lethal, mortal; pestilent: relating to serious and widespread illness or plague

2. lack of movement, staleness, inactivity; stagnation: process of becoming foul or stale from lack of movement

3. to dislike, feel superior to, hate, reject; disdain: look upon something with contempt or scorn

4. to extend throughout, infiltrate, fill up, cover; pervade: spread through every part of

5. impulsive, abrupt, in a hurry, thoughtless, emotional; impetuous: characterized by rash or sudden energy

6. to brag, boast, display, crow, gloat; flaunt: display ostentatiously

7. quiet, gentle, motionless, peaceful; sedate: calm or composed

8. to cut back, reduce, diminish; curtail: cut short, reduce

9. relief; solace: something that gives comfort or relief

10. desirable, irresistible, enchanting; alluring: tempting, fascinating

B. 1. d   2. a   3. b

    4. a   5. c

C. Sample answers are provided.

1. read books, join a discussion group, learn a new language

2. laziness, arrogance, poor grooming

3. neighbor's yard, summer school, the Caribbean

4. drag racing in the parking lot, littering in the cafeteria, talking in study hall

5. angry, envious, disgusted

Lesson 10

A. Accept any reasonable suggestions based on the meanings of the roots, prefixes, and suffixes given. Sample definitions are provided.

1. around the outside

2. severely damaging

3. something out of its proper time period

4. a good death, mercy killing

5. knowledge about one's ancestors

6. person with a diseased mind

7. having human form

8. under the skin

9. ranking with most powerful at the top

10. drying up

B. Sample definitions are provided.

1. outer boundary

2. relating to a serious physical or psychological injury

3. something out of its proper time period

4. putting to death painlessly, "mercy killing"

5. study of family history and ancestors

6. mentally ill person

7. resembling human form, attributing human form to something not human

8. under the skin

9. a system ranking things in order

10. lessening or absence of water

C. 1. anachronism   2. psychopath   3. hierarchy

    4. anthropomorphic   5. periphery

D. Student word webs will vary, but each should show words that have the same root.

Lesson 11

A. Sample definitions are provided.

1. a formal questioning session; roga

2. the act of thinking; cogn

3. detailed, complicated; labor

4. feeling or emotion; sens, sent

5. make something new, introduce changes; nova
6. rich and full in sound; son
7. make an exact written copy; script, scribe
8. fat, obese; corp
9. incapable of being solved or dissolved; sol
10. inactive, at rest; dorm

B.
1. question	2. think	3. work
4. feel	5. new	6. sound
7. write	8. body	
9. loosen or free	10. sleep	

C.
1. dormitory, dormer, dormouse
2. solution, dissolve, resolve, resolution, solve, solvent
3. cognitive, recognize, cognizance, cognate, recognition
4. interrogate, interrogator, interrogatory
5. corps, corpse, corporation, corpuscle
6. laboratory, labor, elaboration, collaborate
7. sentimental, sensitive, sense, sensible
8. novel, innovation, renovate, renovation
9. manuscript, script, scribe, scribble, transcript, scripture, scriptwriter
10. sonar, sonogram, sonic, supersonic, sonata

D. Sentences should use correct grammar and meaningful content.

Lesson 12

A.
1. It is the reference number from the index.
2. *intricate, ornate, laborious, and painstaking* can all be used to describe buildings and the building process, while *complex, complicated, and involved* work better for less tangible artwork such as literature.
3. jolting or shocking; upsetting
4. Look them up in a dictionary.
5. indifference, detestation, dislike, mockery, rejection, scorn, lack of interest

Review: Unit 3

A.
1. b	2. d	3. c
4. c	5. a	6. b
7. d	8. a	9. d
10. a		

B. Sample answers:
1. The interrogation of the prisoner produced valuable information about the crime.
2. The bells in the bell tower played a sonorous melody.
3. The cicadas lie dormant in the ground for 17 long years!
4. Would you please listen to the tape and transcribe the words to the first song?

Test: Unit 3

A.
1. c	2. a	3. c
4. d	5. d	6. b
7. a	8. d	9. b
10. d		

B.
1. d	2. c	3. b
4. a	5. d	

C.
1. a	2. b	3. d
4. c	5. b	

Unit 4

Lesson 13

A. Sample synonyms and dictionary definitions are provided.
1. elastic, able to bounce back; resilient: able to recover quickly
2. prudent, farsighted, shrewd, clever, smart; sagacious: having good judgment
3. poise, on even keel, balance, keeping cool; equanimity: being calm and even-tempered
4. mental toughness, guts, grit, bravery, courage, valor; fortitude: strength of mind
5. darkness, uncertainty, indistinctness, dimness, fuzziness; obscurity: quality of being imperfectly known
6. cheat, distract, trick, con; beguile: to deceive by trickery

7. modest, bashful, retiring; demure: reserved in manner
8. prejudiced, set in one's ways, close-minded; hidebound: stubbornly inflexible
9. upset, riot, agitation, chaos, disorder; tumult: disturbance
10. approve of, commend, acclaim, worship; laud: glorify

B. Sample answers are provided.
1. No, he is probably the most famous athlete in the world
2. Stay calm; decide to study harder next time
3. No, because they have to be extremely outgoing to perform for a crowd
4. Have award assemblies, give prizes, give special privileges
5. No, because they are very skilled at tricking others and know all the techniques of tricking others
6. Possibly, since tensions would run high and referees' calls challenged
7. Students should name someone who is set in his or her ways and justify answers
8. No, ten cents is a very small sum and a tantrum would be an overreaction
9. No, because it is very risky
10. Students will probably say resilient and hidebound, since these adjectives describe opposing personal characteristics. Accept other reasonable choices if justified appropriately.

Lesson 14

A. Sample definitions provided. Students should use correct grammar and meaningful content in their sentences.
1. experimental, hesitant; unsure
2. fearless, courageous; bold
3. to act with condescension
4. something that covers, especially with gloom or darkness; shroud
5. suffering or trial; hardship
6. to hate intensely; despise
7. frankness, honesty; sincerity
8. indirect suggestion, often negative; hint
9. sharply changeable; unsteady
10. to put an end to; stop

B.
1. pall	2. insinuation	3. tentative
4. tribulation	5. candor	6. suppress
7. abhor	8. volatile	9. patronize
10. dauntless		

C. Suggested vocabulary to be used in sentences describing each title:
1. tentative, tribulation	2. abhor, candor, suppress
3. pall, tribulation	4. volatile, dauntless
5. patronize, candor	

Lesson 15

A.
1. ob; hinder, block, get in the way of
2. counter; force opposed equally to another
3. anti; strong feeling of aversion
4. op; oppose, call into question
5. contra; smuggled goods, goods not allowed to be imported
6. ob; intrude, force oneself or one's opinion on others
7. anti; opposite of a stated idea
8. anti; drug like penicillin that destroys germs
9. contra; expressing the opposite
10. pro; one who argues in support of something

B.
1. oppugn	2. proponent	3. contraband
4. antibiotic	5. obstruct	6. counterweight
7. antipathy	8. contradictory	9. obtrude
10. antithesis		

C. Sample sentences are provided. Sentences should use correct grammar and meaningful content.
1. Raising taxes was the antithesis of everything he believed in.
2. Her motives were so noble that no one dared to oppugn them.
3. He received contradictory signals about the location of the target.
4. Martha's practicality provides a counterweight to Jeff's imagination.
5. The drug smugglers denied possessing any contraband.

6. Colleen's tendency to obtrude hinders effective discussion.

7. Senator Bing, a proponent of an active foreign policy, voted for the bill.

8. The antibiotic worked quickly to stop the spread of the infection.

9. The lawyer's goal was to obstruct the court proceedings with as many legal challenges as she could use.

10. I can understand her antipathy for the McCoys—they've been feuding with her family for years.

D. Student responses will vary.

Lesson 16

A. 1. Circle *hen's teeth, fish fur,* or *pig feathers*; meager, lacking in number or amount

2. Circle *I had cheated on the exam, I had used a computer to change my grade*; evil, bad

3. Circle *such famous villains as Ghengis Khan and Attila the Hun*; excessive, especially terrible

4. Circle *hurricane, a flood, a volcano eruption, and an earthquake*; disaster, natural disaster

5. Circle *Denver Broncos, San Francisco Forty-Niners,* and *Green Bay Packers*; threatening, powerful

6. Circle *crushing defeats at Fredericksburg and Chancellorsville*; lowest point

7. Circle *Jimmy Carter, Ronald Reagan,* and *George Bush*; one who came before

8. Circle *Nobel Prize for Literature,* the *Pulitzer Prize,* and *the National Book Award* award; prize

9. Circle *lavish suites, first-class entertainment and meals, half-dozen swimming pools, and, not surprisingly, sky-high prices*; lavish, extremely fancy

10. Circle *country villages, old white churches, and small dairy farms with black-and-white Holstein cows*; quaint, lovely, charming

Review: Unit 4

A. 1. b   2. c   3. d
    4. a   5. a   6. c
    7. b   8. c   9. a
    10. d

Test: Unit 4

A. 1. b   2. a   3. a
    4. d   5. b   6. d
    7. c   8. b   9. c
    10. a   11. c   12. a
    13. b   14. d   15. a
    16. c   17. b   18. d
    19. a   20. b

B. 1. b
    2. c
    3. a
    4. d
    5. b

Unit 5

Lesson 17

A. 1. diligent   2. tantalize   3. adept
    4. confound   5. superlative   6. axiom
    7. delve   8. cumulative   9. complement
    10. unerring

B. 1. diligent   2. axiom   3. complement
    4. confound   5. adept   6. complement
    7. confound   8. superlative   9. adept
    10. cumulative

C. 1. axiom   2. delve   3. tantalize
    4. confound   5. complement   6. adept
    7. superlative   8. diligent   9. unerring
    10. cumulative

Lesson 18

A. 1. b   2. a   3. b

4. d   5. b   6. a
7. b   8. c   9. a
10. d

Lesson 19

A. Sample dictionary definitions are provided.

1. refractory: obstinately resistant to authority or control; resistant to treatment

2. fragment: a small part broken off or detached; to break or separate something into small pieces

3. infraction: a violation of a law or rule

4. frail: physically weak or delicate; easily broken or destroyed

5. osprey: a large fish-eating bird

6. infringe: to trespass or encroach on; to violate or go beyond the limits of

7. fritter: to reduce or squander little by little

8. defray: to undertake the payment of costs or expenses

B. 1. correct   2. defray   3. correct
    4. correct   5. fritter   6. correct
    7. correct   8. fractious

C. Students' paragraphs and example sentences will vary. All three synonyms mean "easily broken" or "damaged." *Fragile* applies to objects not made of strong or sturdy material and requiring careful handling. *Frangible* means capable of being broken but does not suggest inherent weakness. *Frail* applies to things that are physically weak and delicate.

Lesson 20

A. Students' definitions and sentences will vary. Samples are provided.

1. to allay the sorrow or grief of
   Mourners at the funeral could not console the widow and her children.

2. a small storage compartment mounted between bucket seats in an automobile
   In spite of its tiny size, Holly insists that the car's console is for toys.

3. having an abnormally pale complexion
   Rapid breathing and pallid skin are signs of heat exhaustion.

4. lacking vitality; dull
   The action of the play was pallid and the turning point almost nonexistent.

Review: Unit 5

1. b   2. a   3. d
4. a   5. c   6. b
7. a   8. d   9. c
10. d

Test: Unit 5

A. 1. a   2. d   3. b
    4. c   5. d   6. a
    7. c   8. a   9. b
    10. d   11. a   12. c
    13. d   14. b   15. b

B. 1. c   2. a   3. d
    4. b   5. d   6. a
    7. c   8. b   9. c
    10. d

Unit 6

Lesson 21

A. Students' definitions will vary. Sample dictionary definitions are provided.

1. abyss: bottomless gulf; anything too deep to measure

2. agenda: a list or program of things to be done or considered

3. ephemeral: short-lived; lasting for a markedly brief time

4. equilibrium: a state of balance between opposing forces

5. expend: to lay out or use up

6. fortuitous: happening by chance or accident

7. grapple: to try to cope with

8. ideology: a set of beliefs of an individual or a group

9. palpable: easily perceived by the senses; obvious

10. transient: temporary; passing with time

B. 1. fortuitous   2. transient   3. palpable
     4. ephemeral   5. agenda

Lesson 22

A. 1. d   2. a   3. c
     4. a   5. b   6. c
     7. b   8. d   9. a
     10. b

B. 1. serendipity   2. correct   3. vigilant
     4. correct   5. wend   6. ultimate
     7. correct   8. correct   9. correct
     10. correct

C. Students' answers will vary.

Lesson 23

A. Students' definitions will vary. Dictionary definitions are provided.
1. midcontinent: located in the center of a land mass
2. submerge: to place under water; cover from view; obscure
3. circumlocution: the use of unnecessarily wordy and indirect language; evasion in speech or writing; roundabout expression
4. intervention: the act of coming between to modify, settle, or hinder some action
5. substandard: failing to meet a criterion or requirement
6. circumstance: condition or fact attending an event and having some bearing on it; a determining or modifying factor
7. intersperse: to distribute among other things at intervals
8. interact: to act upon one another
9. subconscious: part of the mind below the level of awareness
10. midlife: located in the middle of one's period of existence

B. Students' choices will vary; they might select from among these words:

transcontinental	transform	transfer
transplant	transmit	transport
transit	transact	transposed
peripheral	perimeter	periodontal
peripatetic	perigee	periodic
periscope	advocate	admonish
adjure	adherent	adaptation
adept	ad hoc	

Lesson 24

Students' definitions will vary. Sample dictionary definitions are provided.
1. equivocal: ambiguous; open to interpretation and often intended to mislead
2. disposed: willing
3. pretentious: outwardly extravagant
4. destitute: totally impoverished
5. emboldened: encouraged

Review: Unit 6

1. a   2. d   3. b
4. a   5. c   6. b
7. d   8. b   9. a
10. b

Test: Unit 6

A. 1. c   2. a   3. d
     4. b   5. a   6. b
     7. d   8. c   9. a
     10. d   11. c   12. c
     13. a   14. c   15. d

B. 1. a   2. d   3. b
     4. d   5. c   6. a
     7. c   8. b   9. d
     10. a

Unit 7

Lesson 25

A. Sample synonyms and dictionary definitions are provided.

1. sharpen, taper to a point. whet: to sharpen; make more keen
2. blanch, deprive of color. wan: unnaturally pale; feeble or weak
3. unrewarded, unpaid. unrequited: not reciprocated or returned in kind
4. powerful, able-bodied, mighty. stalwart: strong and sturdy; brave and valiant
5. obliging, unctuous, cultivated. suave: smoothly agreeable and courteous; polite
6. apartness, seclusion, privacy. solitude: state of being alone or removed from others
7. to amuse, to rejoice, to folic. revel: to take great pleasure or delight; make merry
8. thought, meditation, pondering. reverie: a state of abstracted musing; daydreaming
9. to combine, to join. unify: to make into or become a unit
10. disjunction, disconnection. rift: a break in friendly relations

B. 1. solitude   2. rift   3. unrequited
     4. reverie   5. whetted   6. suave
     7. reveled   8. wan   9. stalwart
     10. unify

Lesson 26

A. Students' definitions will vary. Sample dictionary definitions are provided.
1. bigamy: the criminal offense of marrying one person while still legally married to another
2. monolith: a column or monument made from a large block of stone
3. bicuspid: having 2 points or cusps
4. monotheism: the belief that there is only one deity
5. biennial: lasting or living for two years; happening every second year
6. monologue: a long speech made by one person that often monopolizes the conversation
7. bilingual: using or able to use two languages
8. monotony: uniformity or lack of variation in pitch, intonation, or inflection
9. bilateral: having or formed of two sides
10. monogamy: practice of being married to only one person at a time

B. 1. correct   2. monolith   3. bilingual
     4. correct   5. monogamy   6. biennial
     7. correct   8. correct   9. correct
     10. bigamy

Lesson 27

A. Students' definitions will vary. Sample dictionary definitions are provided.
1. prestige: commanding position in people's minds
2. stress: to emphasize, accentuate
3. stricture: an abnormal narrowing of a bodily passage
4. constrict: to compress, squeeze
5. unrestrained: uncontrolled, freed from
6. stringent: marked by money scarcity and credit strictness
7. distress: a state of danger or desperate need
8. constrain: to secure by bonds
9. restraint: a control over the expression of one's emotions or thoughts
10. straits: a situation of perplexity or distress

B. 1. stringent   2. straits   3. constrain
     4. constrict   5. stress   6. unrestrained
     7. strictures   8. restraint   9. prestige
     10. distress

Lesson 28

A. 1. mediocre—moderate to inferior in quality (negative connotations)
     average—of intermediate quality (neutral connotations)
     adequate—sufficient to meet a need (positive connotations)
     2. pleased—glad or contented
     elated—joyful
     ecstatic—enraptured (These three adjectives move from neutral to highly positive connotations.)

B. Student responses will vary.

Review: Unit 7

1. b   2. d   3. a

4. c   5. a   6. d
7. b   8. a

Test: Unit 7

A. 1. c   2. a   3. d
4. b   5. a   6. d
7. b   8. a   9. b
10. a   11. d   12. c
13. b   14. c   15. a
B. 1. a   2. c   3. b
4. d   5. a   6. b
7. c   8. a   9. b
10. d

Unit 8

Lesson 29

A. 1. b   2. c   3. a
4. b   5. c   6. b
7. a   8. d   9. c
10. b
B. 1. a   2. c   3. b
4. a   5. b   6. d
7. b   8. a

Lesson 30

A. 1. affront   2. animated   3. pensive
4. stupor   5. passive   6. nonchalant
7. perseverance   8. accentuate   9. obnoxious
10. perception
B. 1. correct   2. stupor   3. pensive
4. correct   5. correct   6. perseverance
7. perception   8. correct   9. correct
10. correct
C. 1. d   2. a   3. c
4. a   5. b   6. c
7. c   8. a   9. d
10. b

Lesson 31

A. Students' definitions will vary. Sample dictionary definitions are provided.
1. misnomer—an error in naming a person or place; a name wrongly or unsuitably applied to a person or object
2. pseudonym—a fictitious name assumed by an author; pen name
3. nomenclature—a system of names used in an art or science
4. antonym—a word having a meaning opposite to that of another word
5. denomination—one of a series of kinds, values, or sizes, as of currency; large group of religious congregations united under a common faith and name
6. homonym—one of two or more words that have the same sound and often the same spelling but differ in meaning
7. nominal—of, relating to, resembling, or consisting of a name or names; assigned to or bearing a person's name
8. anonymous—having an unknown or unacknowledged name
9. renown—quality of being widely honored and acclaimed; fame
10. ignominy—marked by shame or disgrace; despicable or degrading
B. 1. antonym   2. misnomer   3. nomenclature
4. denomination   5. anonymous   6. renown

Lesson 32

Students' word webs will vary. They might choose from the following synonyms: bravado, opposition, disobedience, insubordination, revolt, rebellion, confrontation, challenge, dare. They might choose from the following antonyms: acceptance, agreement, assent, obedience, submission.

Review: Unit 8

1. b   2. a   3. d
4. b   5. a   6. d

7. a

Test: Unit 8

A. 1. b   2. d   3. a
4. b   5. c   6. b
7. a   8. d   9. d
10. c   11. a   12. c
13. d   14. b   15. b
B. 1. c   2. b   3. d
4. a   5. c   6. b
7. d   8. a   9. a
10. c

Unit 9

Lesson 33

A. Sample dictionary definitions are provided.
1. Students might suggests movies or stories that fit this description. poignant: something emotionally moving or touching.
2. Students might describe a friendly conversation or a meeting with a kind person. benign: kind, harmless, favorable.
3. Students might mention horror movies, Halloween masks, or dilapidated buildings .grotesque: ugly or oddly distorted.
4. Students might mention homes, outfits, or art. Synonyms include flashy, showy, or bright. gaudy: something that is tasteless and flashy.
5. Students might name activities that take place on a balmy day. balmy: warm and summer-like.
6. Students might name scenes in nature or ornate structures. resplendent: glowing and brilliant.
7. Someone who seems unintelligent or dull. obtuse: thickheaded.
8. Students might name everyday objects or activities that fit this description. mundane: commonplace.
9. Students might name pieces of art or designs that they find pleasing. aesthetic: artistic and pleasing to the eye.
10. Students might describe actions that place people in harm's way. wanton: reckless or careless.
B. 1. grotesque   2. benign   3. aesthetic
4. gaudy   5. mundane   6. poignant
7. balmy   8. wanton   9. obtuse
10. resplendent
C. 1. benign   2. poignant   3. gaudy
4. mundane   5. grotesque   6. obtuse
7. balmy   8. resplendent   9. aesthetic
10. wanton
D. 1. poignant   2. benign   3. wanton
4. grotesque   5. aesthetic

Lesson 34

A. Sample definitions are provided.
1. progeny: family; offspring
2. prodigy: genius
3. epithet: slur; harsh name
4. epitaph: words written in honor of someone, especially a deceased person
5. anecdote: a short, entertaining story
6. antidote: remedy; cure
7. apprehend: capture
8. reprehend: criticize
9. vivacious: energetic and lively
10. voracious: large; greedy
B. 1. prodigy   2. epitaph   3. antidote
4. epithet   5. apprehend   6. vivacious
7. progeny   8. reprehend   9. anecdote
10. voracious
C. Students should create with scenes in which a malapropism would cause a great deal of confusion or accidentally insult someone. For example: "You should have heard the epithet he delivered to the crowd at the funeral . . ."

Answer Key

Give students time to brainstorm with their partners. You might have students perform their skits.

Lesson 35

A. 1. chronic: repeating or lasting a long time
2. chronological: sequential, in the order that events occurred
3. synchronize: to begin at the same time
4. chronicle: history or story
5. chronograh: a device used to measure intervals of time
6. synchronicity: the occurrence of events at the same time
7. microfilm: film on which copies of books or documents are reduced and saved.
8. microbiology: the study of microorganisms
9. microscopic: something too small to be seen with the naked eye
10. microbe: a microorganism, such as a germ

B. 1. c   2. b   3. a
4. b   5. b   6. c
7. a

Lesson 36

A. Sample answers are provided.
1. We continued to fret over the lost money.
2. The noise is a continual fret for people in the neighborhood.
3. The designer bordered the room with an attractive fret.
4. I placed my finger on the fret of the guitar and began to play.
5. Did he fret your instrument correctly?

B. 1. young cow–from the Old English word *caelf*; fleshy part of leg–from the Old Norse word *kalfi*.
2. bend the head or body–from Indo-European base meaning "to bend;" anything curved or bent–from Old English word *boga*; front part of a ship–from Swedish word *bog,* meaning shoulders
3. to leap–from Latin *cumbere,* to lie; a type of plant, of German origin
4. to take or keep with hands and arms–of German origin; the interior of a ship
5. the front part of the waist in sitting position–from Latin *lapsus,* "a fall;" to drink, to move or strike gently–from Latin *lambere*

Review: Unit 9

A. 1. b   2. d   3. a
4. d   5. c   6. d
7. b   8. c   9. d
10. c

B. 1. synchronize   2. microscopic   3. chronograph
4. anecdote   5. chronological

Test: Unit 9

A. 1. c   2. a   3. b
4. c   5. d   6. b
7. a   8. d   9. c
10. d

B. 1. a   2. b   3. a
4. d   5. a   6. b
7. b   8. b   9. a
10. d

C. 1. c   2. d   3. c
4. a   5. c

Unit 10

Lesson 37

A. Sample synonyms and dictionary definitions are provided.
1. to pardon, to acquit. absolve: to forgive or clear of guilt
2. to triumph, to succeed. prevail: to overcome, command, or be victorious
3. to deceive, to gyp, to hoodwink. delude: to trick or evade
4. friend, colleague. comrade: an associate or companion
5. devotion, constancy. fidelity: allegiance or loyalty
6. relatives, consanquinity. kindred: having similar ideas or beliefs or related by blood

7. upholder, champion. advocate: a backer or supporter
8. object of compassion, martyr: a person who suffers or even dies for a cause
9. sympathizer, supplicant. partisan: slanted to one side; biased
10. patron, sponsor. benefactor: one that confers kindness

B. 1. benefactor   2. comrade   3. delude
4. fidelity   5. partisan   6. prevail
7. advocate   8. absolve   9. martyr
10. kindred

C. 1. absolve   2. comrade   3. delude
4. fidelity

D. 1. fidelity   2. kindred   3. advocate
4. prevail   5. partisan

Lesson 38

A. Sample dictionary definitions are provided.
1. treachery: deceit
2. arrogance: foolish pride
3. repulse: repel
4. ostentatious: showy
5. sordid: shameful
6. predator: attacker, stalker
7. founder: struggle
8. disconsolate: unable to be comforted
9. solitary: lone
10. caustic: stinging, scathing

B. 1. solitary   2. sordid   3. caustic
4. disconsolate   5. repulse

C. 1. founder   2. ostentatious   3. predator
4. arrogance   5. treachery

D. Students' drawings should show an understanding of the word they choose.

Lesson 39

A. Sample dictionary definitions are provided.
1. emit: to send forth
2. elicit: to draw, gather
3. eminent: celebrated, distinguished
4. empower: to enable
5. evocative: affecting, emotional
6. excise: to dig or pull, remove
7. exposition: writing that explains; a display
8. expunge: to erase
9. exhilarate: to excite
10. expertise: skill and talent

B. 1. d   2. a   3. c
4. b   5. c

C. Students should refer to the meanings of the prefix in the opening paragraph and then explain how the prefix affects the meaning of the word. For example, something evocative calls forth a great deal of emotion.

Lesson 40

1. c   2. a   3. b
4. d   5. c   6. a

Review: Unit 10

A. 1. c   2. d   3. d
4. b   5. a   6. b
7. a   8. d   9. b
10. d

B. 1. ostentatious   2. founder   3. partisan
4. repulse   5. elicit

Test: Unit 10

A. 1. a   2. b   3. c
4. b   5. a   6. d
7. b   8. a   9. c
10. b

B. 1. b   2. c   3. b

Answer Key continued

4. d	5. b	6. a
7. b	8. b	9. c
10. b		

C. 1. c   2. a   3. d
    4. b   5. d

Unit 11
Lesson 41
A. Sample synonyms and dictionary definitions are provided.
1. to oppose, counteract. confront: to come face to face with, especially with defiance or hostility.
2. to surmount, overcome. vanquish: to defeat in battle.
3. valor, gallantry. prowess: superior strength, courage, or daring, especially in battle.
4. valiant, heroic. intrepid: resolutely courageous.
5. plucky, resolute. undaunted: not discouraged or disheartened; courageous.
6. courtesy, urbanity. chivalry: the qualities of an ideal medieval knight, including bravery, honor, and courtesy toward women.
7. philanthropy, humanitarianism. altruism: unselfish concern for others.
8. commendable, meritorious. laudable: admirable; worthy of praise; commendable.
9. to be resolute, to hold on. persevere: to persist in pursuing a goal despite obstacles or discouragement.
10. attempt, venture; to try. endeavor: a conscientious effort toward a goal; an earnest attempt.
B. 1. false; an intrepid cyclist would not be afraid of traffic
2. true; a warrior's main purpose is to defeat the enemy
3. false; to run away from a battle would not be honorable or courageous
4. true; finding a cure for cancer would be praiseworthy because cancer is a leading cause of death today
5. true; people persist in activities that are meaningful to them, even when they meet obstacles
C. 1. correct; to overcome or suppress
2. correct; superior skill or ability
3. incorrect
4. correct; to work with a specific goal or purpose
5. incorrect

Lesson 42
A. Sample dictionary definitions are provided.
1. combatant: one who takes part in armed combat
2. confidant: a person in whom secrets or private matters are confided
3. adherent: one who follows (adheres to) a particular leader or believes in certain ideas
4. incessant: not stopping or ceasing; continuing without interruption
5. luxuriant: characterized by abundant growth
6. coherent: having the quality of cohering; holding together
7. contestant: one who participates in a contest
8. reverent: characterized by reverence or awe; revering
9. exultant: filled with or expressing great joy or exultation
10. indulgent: indulging; characterized by indulgence or pampering
B. 1. adherent   2. incessant   3. combatant
    4. exultant   5. reverent

Lesson 43
A. Sample dictionary definitions are provided.
1. inscribe: to sign one's name or write a brief message in or on something
2. scripture: a sacred writing or book
3. proscribe: to prohibit or forbid
4. prescribe: to set down as a rule or guide
5. scribble: to write quickly without attention to neatness or style
6. manuscript: a book, document, or other composition written by hand or typed; not printed
7. postscript: a message added to a letter after the writer's signature

8. subscribe: to agree in advance to purchase a certain number of issues of a publication, tickets to a series of performances, etc.
9. transcript: a written or typewritten copy, usually of dictated or recorded material
10. inscription: something that is inscribed or engraved with words or letters
B. 1. manuscript   2. scripture   3. postscript
    4. proscribe   5. prescribe
C. sculpture; from Latin *sculpere*, "to carve"; sculpt, sculptor, sculptural, sculpturesque

Review: Unit 11
A. 1. incessant   2. confidant   3. undaunted
    4. proscribe   5. chivalry   6. luxuriant
    7. persevere   8. manuscripts   9. indulgent
    10. confront
B. 1. d   2. b   3. a
    4. c   5. b

Test: Unit 11
A. 1. b   2. d   3. c
    4. c   5. b   6. d
    7. a   8. a   9. b
    10. b
B. 1. b   2. d   3. a
    4. c   5. d
C. 1. c   2. b   3. b
    4. d   5. a

Unit 12
Lesson 44
A. Sample dictionary definitions are provided.
1. droll: amusingly odd; funny in a whimsical way
2. farcical: ludicrous; funny in a broad, exaggerated way
3. slapstick: a form of comedy marked by chases, collisions, and crude practical jokes
4. facetious: playfully joking; humorous
5. witticism: a clever, funny remark
6. satire: a literary work that attacks human vice or folly through irony, derision, or wit
7. parody: a literary or artistic work that imitates the style of an author or work to create a comic effect or to ridicule
8. jocular: marked by joking
9. wag: a humorous or droll person
10. whimsical: marked by whim; involving sudden and capricious ideas
B. 1. a
2. c
3. d
4. c

Lesson 45
A. Sample dictionary definitions are provided.
1. syndicate: an association of people or fir⸺ d to pursue a common goal or promote a common interest
2. symbiotic: relating to a close prolon⸺ ⸺o or more different organisms of different sp
3. syntax: the pattern of formation
4. synthesis: the combining of s
5. symmetrical: having exactly
6. syndrome: a group of sy
7. sympathetic: existing o mutual association
8. synergy: combine
9. synonymous: h⸺
10. synopsis: a c⸺
B. Sample diction⸺
1. sympath⸺

132 Answer Key

2. sympathetic: relating to part of the autonomic nervous system
3. sympathetic: a vibration produced in one body by vibrations in a neighboring body
4. sympathetic: operating through a mutual organization

C. from the Greek *sunopsis,* "general view"; *sun,* syn-, + *opsis,* "view"; other words in family include optic, optical, optometry, optometrist

Lesson 46

A. Sample synonyms and dictionary definitions are provided.
   1. point of view, outlook. perspective: a mental view or inclination; a way of seeing the world
   2. to reflect on, to muse on. speculate: to meditate on or ponder a subject; theorize
   3. ghost, phantasm. specter: a visible disembodied spirit
   4. sagacity, discrimination. perspicacious: of acute mental vision or discernment; keen
   5. prying, reconnaissance. espionage: the practice of spying to gain information about the plans and activities especially of a foreign government or a competing company
   6. future, coming. prospective: expected to happen
   7. perceivable, discernible. conspicuous: easy to notice; striking
   8. devoting attention to oneself. introspection: the examination of one's own thoughts and feelings
   9. reflective attention to past events. retrospective: directed to or recalling the past
   10. pitiable. despicable: deserving to be despised; contemptible

B. 1. false; a perspicacious person would be a keen observer
   2. true; introspection means examining one's own thoughts and feelings
   3. false; conspicuous clothing would make you more likely to be noticed
   4. false; a weather forecast looks into the future, not backward

C. 1. d   2. b   3. c
   4. a   5. b

D. "a comprehensive exhibition or performance of the work of an artist over a period of years"

Review: Unit 12

1. b   2. a   3. b
4. b   5. d   6. a
7. c   8. b   9. d
10. d   11. b   12. c

Test: Unit 12

A. 1. syntax   2. facetious   3. Espionage
   4. parody   5. specters   6. prospective
   7. synonymous   8. synthesis   9. perspective
   10. retrospective   11. satire   12. synergy
   13. perspicacious   14. synopsis   15. introspection

B. 1. d   2. a   3. b
   4. b   5. a   6. c
   7. b   8. d

C. 1. d   2. a